the martyrology
BOOK 6 BOOKS

1978-1985

bp nichol

The Coach House Press Toronto

ISBN 0-88910-319-4

a counting

'One's pestered in these days by so many 'ologies
    We thought we would fain see the tale of our foes;
A niche of your own in the new Martyrologies
    You'd earn if you'd only go halves in our woes.'

author unknown -- quoted in C.C.Bombaugh's *Oddities and Curiosities of Words and Literature*

'If I don't learn to shut my mouth I'll soon go to hell'
– Christopher Okigbo (1932-1967)

these books are

Saint Albans Road
Saint Andrews Boulevard
Saint Aubyns Crescent
Saint Bartholomew Street

Saint Clair Gardens
Saint Clarens Avenue
Saint Cripsins Drive
Saint David Walk

Saint Enoch's Square
Saint Johns Place
San Carmello Way

Christ (i.e. St.)
sections
                inter
pretations
                    pen
etrations
at the corner of
mundane & sacred
snow in my shoe &
dreams of
Who?
of some other, higher, life

Book I

IMPERFECTION: A Prophecy

straight
as the crow flies
arrow

part I

'Salute Andronicus and Junias, my kinsmen, and my fellow prisoners, who are of note among the apostles, who also were in Christ before me.'

Romans 16: 7

·

did you see Him then upon the mount?

we saw Him

and did you see Him then in the hills of Galillee?

we saw Him

·

boat   water   sail

in a corricle over the sea in madness
in a corricle over the sea in grief

'forgive us our tongues of dust our lips of stone forgive us'

under the sun on a blue sea in the salt wind

sail   water   boat

·

skin wrinkle brown hand tiller eye robe
wind skin beard hand brown hair tiller hand
arm wrinkle wind sun eye robe brown skin
sky boat brown tiller robe wind wrinkle eye

·

forgive us for words said forgive us for words unsaid forgive us who loved You silently forgive us the day we failed You Lord forgive us the day we failed ourselves failing You Lord in a boat on the sea under the sun in the sky beyond us forgive us

·

.

so that this way we went & this
that way & back
this way & that
following Joseph

& did you find him

in time yes

& the voyage

yes

.

mistmistmistmistmist
mistmistmistmistmist
mistmistmistmistmist
boatmistmistmistmist
avewavewavewavewav
mistmistmistmistmist
mistmistmistmistmist
mistmistmistmistmist
mistboatmistmistmist
avewavewavewavewav
mistmistmistmistmist
mistmistmistmistmist
mistmistmistmistmist
mistmistboatmistmist
avewavewavewavewav

.

i have not known Thee or loved Thee enough Lord who would seal his lips up against Thee would not make my stand in the marketplace hid back amongst the shadows as they lead Thee away tho You smiled at me let me know You understood the dreadful fear within me which has no place with Thee i have not understood Thy suffering in the simplest terms Lord how You let them know Thy spirit & Thy name how You let them laugh & jeer at Thee firm within Thyself let them kill Thee & did not curse them

i have understood so little Lord in my cringing smallness my weaknesses I have indulged Lord did not understand how they weakened me until they lead You away Lord & i was silent did not strike out did not lead a multitude against them as i should have could have had i but faced the fear & littleness within me

.

rainmistmist
rainmiboatst

raimnistmist
raimniboatst

ramiinstmist
ramiinboatst

rmaiisntmist
rmaiisboatst

mriasitnmist
mriasiboatst

mirsatimnist
mirsatboatst

misrtamiinst
misrtaboatst

mistrmaiisnt
mistrmboatnt

mistmriasitn
mistmrboattn

mistmirsatin
mistmiboatin

mistmisrtain
mistmiboatin

mistmistrain
mistmiboatin

asleep
in a boat
above the deep
waters
waters
waters
waters
waters

.

we have left Thee behind Lord, left ourselves in that leaving, far from truth from being true to Thee, fled, in our fear, over the sea, forever, i can never forgive me, we can never forgive us, the day we fled that last chance to serve Thee

we left us behind Lord, with Thy body, on a cross, saw them hammer the nails in, with the others, so many before You we had watched bleed to death, so many deaths we have spoke against in silence, as we did again, railed against them wtih downcast eyes & turned backs, railed against them & abandoned Thee

.

the waves
against the boat
the waves
against the boat
the waves
against the boat
the waves
against the boat
the waves
against the boat
the waves
against the boat
the waves
against the boat
the waves

.

so where did you go?

this way
& that

&

    only ourselves
crazy in the vast blue of
the sky
the sea

.

sometimes in the night frightened by my own cowardice things i should've said or done dreams the man in black walking towards me the buildings falling i am powerless to stop him tho his face is mine his eyes are mine i am watching it all happen wordless

sometimes in the morning waking the boat is rocking he is watching me & i say nothing i say less & less think more & more my lips dry yes as much from stubborness as lack

of desire set sail in despair into the midst of

at night the dreams of daytime & my silence my inabilities my

.

gulls

gills . (& in the distance hills)

part 2

'having heard the story of the giant Buamundus in the happiness of a feast, jestingly called his son by the giant's name.

Ordericus Vitalis

Historia Ecclesiastica IV, 212
(as quoted in *The Lost Literature*
of Medieval England by R.M. Wilson)

B
U
A
M
U
N
D
U
US

.

being more than most

being of some parts larger
(the girth)

being loud of mouth &
large of appetite

being proud of his size
his strength

B O O !!
set a scare
AMONG US

.

1)myth

2)legend

3)rumour

4)truth

simply no way of knowing

.

.

certain: was talked about

uncertain: what was said

certain: a jest

uncertain: whether he would have thot it funny

.

```
                n t
              u     a
            o         i
BUAM                    NDUS
```

came there
            to that cross

Christianity then
in England
              circa 65 a.d.

among the saints the disciples the crowds that gathered

Andronicus
Junias
Buamundus

·

us as us

history

as in
we have one

remembered

forgotten

all at once &
together

the absence inseparable from the presence

gone so much longer Lord than You were with us

·

being drunk one night
pissed in a stream
overflowed
the whole town flooded

no one would speak of it
fearing they had
wet their beds
a sign
the witches still said
of inconstancy

this & other tales
before his conversion

.

was said to have slept with
various women
                                        possible
as he was
small for his size
(source of some shame
tho for his situation --
lack of other giants --
a blessing)

.

rumoured to have impregnated
all the women in one village
at their request

was actually shy but
in demand

longed for
the company of
ordinary folks

other
people

.

Briefly:
Unhappy
And
Misunderstood
Until
Near
Disciples.
Ultimately (& this stands outside the known pattern) it is their
Story

part 3

'Esperaunce in the worlde nay.
The world variethe every day.

Esperaunce en dieu in hym is all,
For he is above fortunes fall.'

Anonymous 'in the roofe of the hyest chawmbre in the gardynge' at the Duke of Northumberland's house at Leconfield, as quoted in J.G. Russell's *The Field of Cloth of Gold* (London 1969.)

·

night

in the fields under the stars

<pre>
                    sleeping

                      sleeping

                        sleeping
</pre>

·

<pre>
          Andronicus
                                   shadow
                                     stone

                        shadow   shadow
                          stone   stone

      shadow   shadow
           stone   Junias   stone

  shadowstone   shadowstone

          stone   stone
     shadow   Buamundus   shadow

              stone   stone
          shadow   shadow

                               stone
                            shadow
</pre>

.

circle

        stone

                    circle

        cross

stone

        cross

                    circle

        cross

circle

        stone

.

              &

              u
              p

        across & across

              d
              o
              w
              n

              &

.

.

three

one + ONE + one

equals

.

we sing Thy praises Lord, talk endlessly of Thy sacrifice

Thy greatness Lord is sung of in this far land by many who never knew You in Your humanness, Your frailties

we are shadows Lord, cast out from Thee, fallen upon this distant shore among other shadows, Your orchads

our voices echo over the rocks & trees & in our echoing Lord we praise Thee

.

but did you see them upon the mountain tops?

no

or in the hills of Albion?

no

•

gone & forever gone

gone without hope of returning

gone in human body gone

into death into heaven into

gone beyond reach of talking

gone beyond reach of singing

in our prayers

listening

the wind

the leaves

bird songs
among the shifting, creaking

•

were said to have
visited many villages
preaching

a sight
remarkable for
its strangeness

Andronicus
depicting Buamundus as
a convert from
the ranks of
the Green Man
who now declared
Christ & Jehovah
greater than
the deities & godlings of
these parts

tho many questioned the effectiveness of
one prayer one God
whether He could
possibly answer them all
(most having come from large families)
the idea
took hold

.

some rumours of
strange encounters in
these times

a woman
returning home late
saw the giant
naked dancing in a field
accompanied by
three equally naked
girls

Buamundus
declared another giant
guilty
        tho none were known in
        those parts

·

certain: nothing

uncertain: they converted many of the small villages & isolated holdings in the southwest of most of what was then Britain

certain: by 75 A.D. christianity had spread thru most of Britain

uncertain: what these three had to do with it.

·

66
67
68
69
70
71
72
73
74
75
76
77
78
79
80
81
82
83
84
85 a.d.

a description then, some listing of their last years, their deaths

from here

↑

of these

this

↓

part 4

'*bran*, crow

bran vras, raven

bran dre, rook'

from *A CORNISH-ENGLISH DICTIONARY* edited by Morton Vance

. (some history sketched)

```
              JOB
        S     O .
  L HAGIOGRAPHY C
  AGE O NO  A   .
  WORLD  DEITIES
-------------------
   DEUS IS  O  A.D.
     S      N  V
CHRIST      CHRIST
    I      HE  O
    N          U
               R
```

. (a sermon: fragments)

did this thing as i have told you of which if there is any man or woman can say different step forward

---

so in my grieving it came to me a penance i could do in this world for he who tries to enter into heaven shall open the gates of hell you must renounce your claim on heaven to enter it you must enter into this world to claim heaven

---

take up our words as we took up His your conviction convinces others of His words

---

do not be quick to rebuke or condemn lest in the words leaving your lips you echo yourself

. (geography)

unknown   ocean   britain

↗

some islands
in between
this ⟶
⟵ & that

east
the sun rises

west
the sun sets

↖

∴ death &
the afterlife

journeys
into   the spirit world

. (a prophecy)

above
the village
atop the hill
these things said:

we will not see it in our lifetime nor in our children's lifetime nor in the lifetimes of their children's children but in the time of all their children this loving & this forgiveness will be everywhere until we will have founded the peaceful Kingdom God intended for us in this world

. (a further geography [hindsight])

the unknown
was/is
(at least partially)
Canada

later
'The New World'
where
'the streets were
paved with
gold'

        (trace memory of
         the afterlife
                        Valhalla
         heaven
                  the world of
                  faerie

over the North Atlantic

(a voyage)

the owl &
the pussycat &

. (the reasoning)

there were rumours or
legends

          'the lands beyond
           the lands we know'

peopled
it was supposed

a further penance

because they (Andronicus [the owl] &
Junias [the pussycat]) could not
know peace in this world nor (possibly)
heaven (in another)

set out with
Buamundus

no maps

under a yellow sun
in a green boat
on a blue sea

. (details)

pillars
of shimmering glass

(in fact
more pyramidal
in shape &
made of ice)

islands of
fire in
the cold

(volcanic)

monsters

(whales, etc.)

wind & sea

(wind & sea)

. (flashback)

Andronicus
seized the opportunity for
a last

sermon

gathering
the villagers on
the beach (mostly
rocks tho
some small pebbles)
addressed them from
the boat where
the three travellers
sat

much joking in
the crowd about
how Buamundus might
sink the ship with
his weight

the theme
Andronicus chose: 'how
faith
keeps us afloat'

. (more details)

↑

headed north

← in order to go west

(rumours

an island

dotted lines on the few extant maps

....

. (theories)

known (sort of): a giant
slept on
an island in
the North Atlantic
Brendan
discovered
awoke &
lent him a hand
circa 500 a.d.

unknown (really): whether
he was
Buamundus

---

theory 1: Buamundus
quarreled with
Andronicus &
Junias
somehow
thrown overboard
survived on
that island
400 years &
more (the
lifespan of
giants
not being known)

theory 2: Buamundus
requested to be
let out

BUAMOUTNDUS

stands guard over
this bleak region
assisting Christian travellers on
their quests

theory 3: an older giant
Chronos
slept there

Buamundus knew this &
avoided the island
having heard the legend as
a child
a century or more
before

theory 4: none of the above

. (maps)

B
R
I
T
A
I
N

(t
h
e
n)

the boat ↖ the
boat

the boat ← the
boat

↙ the boat

C
A
N
A
D
A

(n
o
w)

---

none of this was (of course) recorded

. (biographical note)

variants exist
(the same information
juggled differently)

viz: Bron
the castrate fisher king
who sleeps
& guards the grail

Bran
(Chronos by another name)
on that island
sleeping

Bren-
dan as
mentioned

Brun
(portmanteau
-- an older god in
these parts [i.e.
Canada])

all the above
linked to
the Sleeping Giant
(Lake Superior,
Thunder Bay)

Buamundus

Bua being
possible variant spelling of
Bron &/or Bran
mundus
the world &
being as he was/is
a world figure
        (again
            Atlas
        Bran/Chronos by a 3rd name)
        held the world on
        his shoulders

formulaic spelling = $\frac{\text{mundus}}{\text{bua}}$

i.e. bua is under
in the under world

the underworld carries
the world on its
back

Faerie &
the Isle of Avalon
(where Bron sleeps)
etc. etc.

these
& other
probable systems

facts

. (the unknown)

boat
<u>shore water</u>

Q: what shore?

Q: which boat?

(this
the whole question of
discovery
i.e.
'Who's on first?')

Q: who's in the boat?

(one + one + ?)

Q: which body of water?

. (the gravity of the situation)

earth relative to the sun

the sun
relative to
the galaxy's heart

both rotating

the galaxy
relative to
other galaxies
forming a larger cluster

still rotating

the whole thing   moving outwards
from a central point or probable beginning
no longer perceivable

parallel: the soul/self
relative to
the body

the body
relative to
some companion's heart
(family/lover/friend)

both revolving
/changing

relative to
other people
forming larger units of selves
(neighbourhoods/towns/cities/etc.)

still changing

the whole thing
everyone
growing older &
dying
        from a central point or
beginning
no longer perceivable

application: miles from anywhere
    in terms of
    the known
        in terms of
    a language or
    cultural grouping
    the two or
    three of them of
    mixed racial &
    tribal origin
    moving too far outward from
    their centres to
    even perceive them

. (possible scenario)

Buamundus is with them. They travel inland along a huge waterway, thru vast lakes, past giant moving walls of water, to a final landing on a tree covered shore. Here Buamundus falls asleep (this being a common disease with giants (numerous incidents recorded)) & cannot be awakened. Andronicus & Junias continue on. They move south &, as old men, find their way among the Mayans (carvings of men with semitic noses having been discovered in Mayan ruins). No record of their preaching is preserved nor is their death recorded. Buamundus sleeps to this day.

. (another scenario)

Travelling inland they discover the Sleeping Giant (their second). Careful not to wake him they continue westward, Buamundus building scattered circles of earth & stone along the way (such being found in Ontario, Alberta (possible proof of a return to earlier beliefs on Buamundus's part)). Eventually Andronicus & Junias part ways with him (his views seeming, to them, heretical). Buamundus wanders north, falling asleep, is frozen, eventually, his body drifting out to sea (deep source for the Frankenstein legend or, latterly, The Thing &/or the Captain America of the 1960's). Andronicus & Junias travel over the rockies to the west coast & once more set out to sea. Here all surmises become too entangled in tribal variants for even a tentative outline to have any validity.

. (addition)

the facts:

a) names of
Andronicus &
Junias (more
commonly spelt
Junia)

b) early founding of
the Christian church in
England
(Claudius'
decree in
42 a.d. to
snuff it out)

c) name of
Buamundus

d) reference to
the sleeping giant in
Grail legends &
the legend of
Brendan

e) the Sleeping Giant,
Thunder Bay, Lake
Superior, Ontario,
Canada
(visible from
the front porch of
my childhood home)

f) various myths
too numerous to
mention

what it all adds up to

. (the end)

Andronicus -- apostle ⟶ ?

Junias -- apostle ⟶ ?

Buamundus -- giant ⟶ ?

the known guessed at

thus conclusions
&/or theories
viz: science & history
myth & legend
some sense of
the components of
reality

religion being
a combination of
<u>the real</u>
(i.e.
re(a)l)
& <u>the region</u>

formulaic spelling = re(a)l + <u>r</u>egion

= re^2(a)lgion

where (a) = the fleeing centre
the probable beginning

barely perceived
translated (nonetheless) as
'i'
self at the centre

makes re^2(al)lgion = re^{2}ilgion

the 2
drops away
over the
years
(lack of
a written tradition to
preserve it) &
the i shifts
yielding

<u>religion</u>

a region of the real

uncharted
(largely)

open to
misconstruction &
fanaticism
which does not yield to
science or
history (in that
sense)
thru which
the named shadows of
Andronicus, Junias & Buamundus
flicker
but are never glimpsed

1978-79

Book II

A BOOK OF HOURS

for Michael Ondaatje

Hour 1
10:35 to 11:35 p.m.

met a physic
on the road
asked him

so it is with journeys one is drawn

moon & sun
earth & stars

larger figures &
rhythms

our hours

collections of random thots or
meditations

med a tation
on de road
ast him

cold reason

sick in bed X days

viz: this poem or altered consciousness
NOT alerted consciousness

alert to the moment's movement in this room
language is the inside of the head or
the mouth opens

i *feel* that

comparisons between various earthly states

i.e. <u>life death</u>
unhappy happy

you know <u>CATEGORIES</u>

gory cats
in his hats

do you like
my hat?

i do not like (as in *bad* grammar)
i.e. i don't do it like (for purpose of
comparison (comparidaughter))
birth
other minor jokes

not to be confused with
cynicism or
cinemacism

making the right mov-
ie

'They're all watching me!'

paranoia or
the old narcissus bit

word drift

wordrobe

wandering thru the clothes closet of
the (brain?
no!) memory

'this fits me
this doesn't'
throwing out the pants that
you bought
age 23

visions of poetry

H {
a particular voice

particular obsession

confused with posession

First Saint: Who was that?

Second Saint: Last night?

life is continual moods
progressions of
the self

↖ selves

little s elves
viz: the usual language play
access to the world of faerie

the real rhythm is
the rhythm of the hours
progression of the days
years you have left for your

utanikki
(cf. The Martyrology Bk V)

what the hell
it is
after all
a long* work

(*for 'long' read 'continual')

-- looking for ways to give it up?)

so much for
the subjective voice

March 27th
1689
Basho leaving Edo

February 11th
1979
a pen still marks time
pursues the same
insight out

(difficulties of the journey -- records of dead friends -- Frank this year -- Carl & Mark so long ago -- others ahead? -- the seasons -- coincidences of nature & the mind)

this time everything rhymes

a bullet in the head &
a broken heart

art?

i'm just rolling
track '79
the old straight line
narrative
to the deep north
the wood door too
turning into
a wall

what is
'the easy way out'?

definition of electric poetry: 'He's just plugging in!'
definition of a collection of electric poetry: 'He's just plugging along.'

art: do you have to 'like' it?

what changes the world is
the world changing

simple ideas

(it would be nice, for instance, if everybody really did love one another i.e. no more of this sentimental bullshit, idealizing of the thighs, breasts, cock, etc. of the beloved)

on the other hand -- what about 'realism'?

(for 'realism' read 'negative sentimentality')

as if everything depended on
the little brown stool

yuko -- the temporary, changeable element

jitsu -- the substance

kyo -- the essence

Nikko
March 30th 1689
lodged in an inn at
the foot of
the mountain
(wrote poems)

Nichol
February 11th 1979
mounted on his foot at
the in stant
dis lodged
(writing poems)

290 years of
past tense
(approximately)

jitsu -- kyo -- ryuko

continuing the search for
absolute moments of
existence

'let me get this straight'

kyo -- ryuko -- jitsu

<u>THE FURTHER ADVENTURES OF...</u>

...clutching the panting saint to his heaving breast. 'What is the secret?' he gasped.

Saint Orm grabbed his arm &, twisting around, threw him over his hip onto the floor. 'This is the secret!' he snarled.

various faces in the shrubbery

various voices crying to get out

this is
the human condition -- we're
all looking for
release

P = O + 1 = E + 11 = T - 4 = R - 2 = Y - 9

or

16 = 15 + A = 5 + K = 20 - D = 18 - B = 24 - I

a kiss dream build i (me)

give to a on
which is the poem
the hour

rotation of the earth
relative to the sun

'I have an houres talke in store for you'
(William Shakespeare, *Julius Caesar*)
which is to say
i have put it away
behind me

a translation only
no conclusions no

the number of lights still on in the apartment building across the way
is less than when this poem began

24 or so then

now 8

'the hour is getting late'

'its nice to finish something
on time!'

Hour 2
2:35 to 3:35 p.m.

'temperature irregularly high recently'

'he's in heat'

Here
in this too (paper)
is the parcel of hours:
the poems.

relax

into yourself

no images at all

some awareness of neural activity

these are the daily doldrums
the still ness at the centre of
nothing moves
the her again

some shifts as the real drifts into focus

mmmmmmmm

i.e. I
ME
MYSELF
JE
MOI-MEME
etc.

maybe one just drifts off to sleep

              SILENT

                        such a noisy word

May 10th 1899
Masaoka Shiki
sick in bed

                            May 11th 1899
                            behind the fallen peonies
                            Basho's face!

                                                  February 12th 1979
                                                  in two day's time
                                                  my record in verse!

my grandmother was 14 when Shiki wrote his lines

these things

              'the face of the earth'
'an ear to the ground'
                          'the bowels of the earth'
mother

          -- walk all over her body
          never quite
          get her
          together

-- nature

-- earth

              Shiki in his bed

              210 years earlier
              Basho
              walking the back road

never quite get her together

'if you drive the freeways you miss the view'

choose to
walk all over her body like
a metaphor like
a simile

assimilated into her skin at death

wander-
tutor-

inging

bell in the head at dusk each night
pray for light to come
insight
ttttone

art yr oooooooooooo

a rift in
the earth's crust

flakey

pie-eyed at
the world

logic ____
logy

a whole word

(this is a large task -- i.e. collecting all potential signifieds. why bother? you are looking for a whole word, one that contains all its meanings. i.e.:

QUESTION AS HYPOTHESIS

what makes them mean ings if they're theoretically content?

$\therefore$ meaning $\neq$ content

'what is the mean ing of life?'
i.e. the middle ing
(as in sings)

surely not this meaning
that i hear

'he meaned a lot
& then he died'

'the earth
swallowed him up'

(mouth to mouth
& no resucitation))

'with my temperature irregularly high recently'

not a martyr
only logy

makes it hard to
get her together

gathering

steam

'a life of it sown'

'couldn't stop dreaming of roaming,
roving the coast up & down'

slower

slowed

at the still time
the brain rhymes different paths

ganglia

synapses

'There is this silence
About the sickbed'

Q: How can the real be out of focus?
A: Easy!

THE REAL: Act I Scene II:

. . . .

selected hours
framed by
silences

. . . .

(i.e. love, work & other non-writing)

Historical Q: did you
get well soon
Masaoka Shiki?

Hour 3
1:35 p.m. to 2:35 p.m.

history rhymes
time's a vision

---

the sea
gulls &
billows

---

day stretches on if
the road never bends

} EPI grams / cs

here

there

almost everywhere perception gathers

life leads &
steps on
your toes

the ship rolls with
'but her'
'but him'
'and'

conversations

what do you do
if someone interrupts you?

five minutes lost from
the poem

five minutes found for
a life

so what your saying is
& keeps on ising

(islands in mist -- white caps thru a hedge of hairy heads --
rainy panes of glass -- back in B.C. this A.D.)

every poem is simply the history of a writing

what i am most aware of are
the contradictions

'if you can't heckle a Canadian poet
who can you heckle?'
-- anonymous *West Coast Literary Presses Benefit Reading*
February 23rd 1979

everything is coinci & dense

EPI centres
EPI sodes

why do we have to
'get it together'
yeah yeah

tele GRAMS
ana GRAMS

thot is always a crisis centre

'the facts is the facts'

A. I must
B. Go down to the
C's (again)

pound for pound

that old narwhale cissus
blows it out his
blowhole

its the top of my head
ringed in clouds

'he's looking a bit peakèd lately'

tension

ocean

passion

'let me get this strait'

you're looking for
the opening when
the skull is

the five senses
four sight
three nody
two 'n
one
whistles

sea skulls wings at
the windows

EPI calls & culls
you got to
answer

1. the low cull
2. the long distance cull

EPI logue
cure

dis
traction

dis
hold the
actions has on
the brain of

dis traction

waves on rocks

waves in the car

waves in the window as you move farther away from her

vague pronoun references of memory

'you remember Epi!'
'who?'

wave ring the boat

wave ring heart

wave ring image of the selves start their focus

'that son of a bitch <u>really</u> focus!'

for us

the sea

mother

EPI
sea
sodes

margin redraw

everywhere the language gathers

father

famili ar(e

spells spill
out of land's cape we
disembark on

Hour 4:
9:35 to 10:35 a.m.

absolute absence of horizon

viz: a jumble of rooftops &
branches of trees

up to my knees in needs

nothing to do with anything but
the urge to
continue

as a continent

as an edge of land or
sea

time: its all changing even as i look at it

'the old neighbourhood just isn't the same'

'he doesn't write the way he used to'

THE LANGUAGES OF

PAO of
one man
changing

i don't mean English

'A man must try to whip order into
a yelping pack of
probabilities'

'Time advances,
conditions change.'

older by the minute
minuter by the hour

big hand
little hand
which hand has
the pea

a shell game

shuck your body &
leap
into eternity

The Mathematics of Sex
i.e. one into one makes two
sometimes

'she takes math control pills'

viz: one into one makes zero

'put some lead in your pencil'
or you can't write the future

's changing

he can't get his clock up

automatic
mathematic
traumatic

ma in the attic
comedy

stepped from her body into time

clock sucker
gives it the head

'get the lead out'
(now its slowing him down)

trying to reach the edge

Scene 1:
A busy street about 10 in the morning. St Reat is walking by. Captain Poetry addresses him.

Captain Poetry:

Cigarette?

St Reat:
(patting his pockets)

Sorry.

Captain Poetry:

Match?

St Reat:
(patting his pockets again)

Sorry.

Captain Poetry:

Time?

St Reat:
(rolling up his sleeves to show his empty wrists)

Sorry!

SKILL TESTING QUESTION: In the play you have just read, was St Reat correct in his last statement?

---

one into one makes someone
dramatic

Scene 2:
St Orm is winding his watch. We hear a crunch & a sproing.

St Orm:

Whoops! Damn! Wound it too tight.

St Ranglehold:
(entering the room)

Something wrong?

St Orm:

My watch is broken!

St Ranglehold:
(taking a watch out of his pocket)

That's okay. I can keep time.

rhythms

the clock ticked
his heart thumped
his heels clicked

'let's just drop the whole thing'

tick
thump
click

'i don't have time for this sort of bullshit'

thump
click
tick

'we could save time by forgetting about it'

click
tick
thump

t hump
c lick

i.e. The Alphabetics of Sex

correction
direction
erection

'i want some ection!'

'time's come!'

Scene 3:
St Raits wanders down a busy street. A man in tudor costume passes by. Another man, dressed like a caveman, & a third man, dressed like an astronaut, also pass him.

St Raits:
(pausing to scratch his head as they pass)

What time is it?

langu age
old age
p age

static

interference at the edge of space & time

light years
'the best years of our lives'
image travelling on
too small to
focus on

science fiction or
fictional science

Probable Systems

tricks with time

5/4 4/4 3/4

scores between the left hand & the right

sleight of hand

muse
music
museum

artifacts
art facts

pitch, melody &

'he's ahead of his time'

'they did it all in Moscow in the 1920's'

derivative
dervish or

ECSTATIC

'doing it at the hourly rate'

'thank you.
i had a good time.'

Hour 5:
8:35 to 9:35 a.m.

so it is the journey draws us

or sometimes the return

miles of flat land and
diffused grey blue cloud at
the horizon

clusters of farm buildings
little clumps of trees

sketches

the eye catches
details

stark white garage or
henhouse
greyed farmhouse behind

earth

it turns beneath us

sky

envelops us

space

all around us

us is very small
very tiny edge detail
almost invisible factors in the universe

Zelma

one grain elevator

almost invisible i's eye

almost invisible eye

a life

it passes

earth covers us in &
in time forgets us

tiny graveyard

weatherworn stone

Poe's in Baltimore

Steve, Kirby, Marshall & me
visiting (November '78)

smashed tombstones

cracked mausoleum

Poe's grave moved
closer to the gate
because of
the number of visitors
came to see him

him's gone
hers gone

hymns as the hearse drives us away

us's all we's

black earth with
a sprinkling of
white snow

ice coated wire fences
white glare rectangular outlines
white glare bushes pushing up thru snow

we never dies

racial memory confused with heaven
confused with reincarnation

a landscape in time

pick your way thru the shifting faces
drifting places of memory

'they tore the old schoolhouse down'

or like Ellie
returning to Bay Trail, Saskatchewan
they'd taken all the buildings away
even the sign

'the town i was born in no longer exists'

a line of telephone poles

wires

a line (shorter) of trees

Bradwell

one elevator

'we need more space'
'we need less space'
'people need space to grow in'

pale yellow stubble of frozen wheat
darker brown gold of the gravel road
stripped red of the barkless telephone pole

linear movement of train thru space & time
strange drift of passengers thru memory

'i recognize this place'

see is the seed for seen

jumble of corrugated steel
ten tin silo tops
tips tilted at the train

everything depends on
the red cultivator
unmoving in the gold white field
(a statement of the fall)

loose a fir
gain a pine

lonely without you or (worse)
lonely with you

the couple in the next roomette
always together tho they don't talk
tho they're both cramped

lonely why?

someone's definition of hell

'saturday night is the loneliest night of the week'
'gloomy sunday'
'monday morning i feel bad'

weekness

'they want to be buried together'

'they were so close --
when he died she lost the will to live
died three months later'

a grave yard
a happy yard
a yard on down the road

a lumber yard by the side of the tracks

they bury you two yards down

sometimes
its your first
permanent address

Poe moved after death
for the convenience of
his uninvited guests

a journey from this world to the next
with stops along the way

QUEEN ELIZABETH POWER STATION
heading into the train station
i'm trying to pick up the local station
i'll wait until we're stationary

'don't stand still or they'll kill you'

'if you lie down once you'll never get up again'
cover you in

under earth

under sky

a place somewhere in space

very small
very tiny
very (for all intents & purposes) invisible

circling

rotating

very stationary in the Saskatoon station

'that's the situation
in a nutshell'

'good things come in small packages'

space

invisible in the crowd flowing from the train

seen but unrecognized
unknown

sitting in the station

stationary in the sitting room

that's the situation
the sitcom

very tiny moment
insignificant day

visible invisibility

tiny spot at the galaxy's edge
tiny galaxy in the universe ahead & around us

th-that's it

even after the end

th'that's all
folks

Hour 6:
4:35 to 5:35 a.m.

sick in bed (three days)

temperature irregularly high recently

awakened from dream from
the image shuffle
snow on the ground
beyond the door
's all night

sap run from the maple trees in buckets

's all night

wind thru the crack in the door

's all night

moaning

crying

is it the dream image
the wind in the door
the

whole nights drift on without you
alseep & tossing into dream or
nightmare ride across the field of thot

the world turns on without you
without your words

houselights out all up the 7th line
only the barnyards lit
horses & the cows asleep

animal land

mouse & skunk & rabbit asleep

the dream pushed me out
pulled me up   into the waking world

'everyone's asleep'

a signal

toys come to life

mice
move out along the empty halls
paws clutching their tiny tails
'don't make a noise, don't wake them'

awake

the living & the dreaming

'he (the rat) is jealous of my poetry...
he was a punk poet himself
and after he has read it sneers
and then eats it'
Archy

awake

the memory & the memoried

'magic words of poof poof piffles
make me just as small as...'

sniffles

awake & breathing

whole lives drift by
untouched by your feelings
your presence

along the hall
towards the kitchen

light thru
the crack in
the fridge door

'the cat's asleep'

whole centuries drift by
you are not alive
your thots unrecorded
unremarked
unneeded

animal hands

animal faces

animal feelings
at the base of
the brain
drawn from
in sleep

millenia gone
millenia to come

tiny whiskered faces
whispers in the chill light of
the room

this is the dream time

you are one year old

you want to go where
the animals go

in fever forever
always in heat

every day the store of images increases

every day your vocabulary varies

hunting for food in the long halls
past the sleeping cats
across the waxed & polished floors

every night the brain throws them up again
shuffle from childhood forward

awaking startled
awaking so slow you forget

awaking mid images of dreamed sex
tongues touching
fingers on the nipples breasts & cock

down the corridors of dreamed houses
pursuing the longed for face or body
absolute moment when the mind loops back on itself
eyes closed to the world beyond

                                        animal longings

enveloping sex

swift part & clench of too soft lips

                                          's all night

awake excited
frightened

that close to
the bidden

forbidden

          animal heat
          in the cold night drift

unfocussed fear

unfocussed desire

the inner & the outer worlds

                                      'the turtle lives
                                       twixt plated decks'

                                       animal strangeness in
                                       the long corridors of
                                       the house

lights out

staring out the window
white glare snow
5:20 a.m.
not yet dawn &
the wind blow

this is the dream time
in heat in the cold

quick click of teeth &
lick of whiskers

whole days drift on without you
sick in bed or
lost in a fever dream

so familiar motion
in & out of
her dreamed body

animal time

drifts on without you

the days are passing memories

so familiar feeling of
desire

's all night
awake now

whole hours drift by without you

longing
(in the dream)
for the self
(really)

one animal flow thru
the whole body

drifts by without you

asleep
you watch it go
sailing over the fences
the snowy fields
above the caves & homes of animals

out you

Hour 7:
11:35 p.m. to 12:35 a.m.

powerless all day

loading logs into the truck
snow cling the thwuck & thunk
driving back & forth
one house to the other
thru the valley
over the hill
hook up the generators for the greenhouses
save the plants
amid the wind
whistle & the crunch of
snow breaking under boots
around the lips
lighting the candles as night falls
gather 'round the fire
talk of storms

'same time of year in '75
snowed in 3 days
claustrophobia drove her crazy'

'a pleasant day
drifty &
strange'

snow & the wind

pushing

breathless

falling forward
feet first
into

you spend the whole day waiting for the wind to stop
moving

less

pushed on
tho you're not

routines forgotten/
/schedules changed
the wind drove us all day
scurrying back & forth
arms full of wood
of food

of the mind's workings &
the heart's

all our life the heart drives us
furiously into the arms of lovers
crying & desperate
laughing & sane
arms full of

each other we contain contains us

wind blew furiously
lifted the snow
blew in walls of white against the glass
shudder in the frame & strain

the body aches & is full of longing
the broken limbs crashing
half way over the road
driving by
head stuck out the window
white out

loss

of vision

of the heart's working

the thingness of things

in storm

in heat

the fire in the grate glows
coals shift into ash
the crumpled pages flare & are gone

so slow

so very very slow

even tho the wind blows & the breath comes in gasps
the heart races
everything moves so slow

impossible memory trace

flicker & gone

the day's slow as glass

passes into the night yawning

all night the generators roll
taking it in shifts
feeding the gas
in darkness
under the falling snow

wind blows
slower & slower

all your life your heart pulls you
longing takes you
one state of mind to

another

self

so many many

burst thru the thots swirl towards you
out of the minds of strangers yet unborn
white wall of the future moving forward

goodbye

this world to another

mid night & dream &

the scene is strangely the same

goodbye

moves past you & is gone

wind

slower & slower

takes you

take me

the hour of almost cold
when the few lights flicker
the candles burn low

& the wind

the moving air

around you
the selves flicker

the hour of not quite there

out of the nursery rhymed

icker fl icker fl icker fl ight 'n
the many within the one skin float
tenses overlapping

present & past

the wind blows

all around you

slower &
slower

the selves fold
back in the image shuffle

the hour before you dream

crying & desperate
laughing & sane

all your life desire fills you
white of her flesh swept towards you

in the night

in the hour of animal heat

in the sweet surrender of the flesh
love takes you   utterly
swept forward on the flood
out of
            into

                    selves

like a

             as if

                        only itself

as the wind blows

as all around you frozen branches creak
the snow
             presses thru the screens
splatters against the glass
drifts shaping/
                /reshaping
hour after hour
as you watch
as you turn away
without you
despite you
unconnected to

                        anything

in the hour of absolute

                                only itself

wind & snow

                    across the road
                    into the trees
                    swirling
                    flake to flake

impossible memory trace

                                drift & are gone

the night's slow as glass

passes into the new day yawning

powerless

only the generator's roar
as creak of stairs
as you passes thru the many many rooms
so many doors & windows to choose

only itself

& the wind blows

slower & slower

slowed

down

the snow falls
over the frozen
soon to be planted

you heart ground selves wind snow

Hour 8:
4:35 to 5:35 p.m.

lost

Hour 9:
7:35 to 8:35 a.m.

'and a river went out from Eden'
into the world

East

the sun

the mind

barely awake

into the rising
which is the world turning

day

on the sea wall

shadow falling   west   over the sand

among the palm trees & the brush

fish   leaping up

'all the time in the world'

out there   in the gulf
nets spread
floats bob on the flickering surface

all the time in

'& time out'

tide

feet in the shifting surf   surface   of the world

almost the end of
the second millenium
since Your son's birth

are we Your children?

in Your image?

i'm age

a natural process then death
no questions of a heaven or a second life

'you've got to take a...'

'chances are'

the river leads on
into a lake or

ocean

circling

gulls

sand

pipers

against the sea wall

pelicans

the moving air

breathing

in & out

(meditations on
the world

asked Him)

'the way of...'

i'm age & aging

the body loses its elasticity

muscles sag

sages

'How much time have we got?'

the wages of

he rages at his own mortality
she rages at her own mortality

running out

low tide

approaching

receding

at the edge of

'with you in a moment'
'only got a minute'
'only take a minute'
'wasting my time'

against the ear drums

among the shifting
pressed against

'world enough &...'

'no time like the present'

none at all

as the waves fall on the beach &

birds call

back & forth

over the sea

'as good a time as any'

out of Eden into the world

'Lest the awe should dwell
And turn your frolic to fret
You shall look on my power at the helping hour
But then you shall forget!'

(in this absence

in this silence in the brain
when no words come

only the acknowlegement of
presence

talking tho i've no right to think You're listening

'at the helping hour'

at the edge of the great salt river circles the world

under the fragile blue dome of air encloses us

breathing

in &

'...out from Eden'

'and a river went...'

Hour 10:
10:35 to 11:35 a.m.

bitten.   horsefly buzzing 'round my ears

on a rock
above the raspberry canes

blueberry bushes pushing thru the cracks

mosquitoes

wild hay &
skunk cabbage

'bitten by the urge'
'the writing bug'
something
at my right shoulder

bird calls   high
followed by two low   & short
notes

outside history

what freedom is

tyrannies opposed
bitter wars   (THE OUTRAGE)
whole peoples displaced   (DESTROYED)

finally takes its place in
the natural world

outside all will to power

Chiang K'uei
Su T'ung Po

perceptual sets
not unlike my own

words on paper
as the world around
ebbs & flows

madness

dark dreams of death &
mutilation

dragonflies &

all around you
fields stretch on
the fence lines run

daisies

one outcrop to
another

wings of
monarch butterflies

around you
the curtain of air falls
more people every day
dying
than even your wish to
can encompass

old age

starvation

sickness

war

around you
the bushes yield their fruit
the buzz of grasshoppers or
cicadas

outside memory where
the land exists

buildings crumble

steeples that were raised to heaven
fall

green fluttering wings of
white fluttering wings of

butterflies

over the fields

birds & beasts call

trying to connect it all
impossible brief perspective of the present

ALL

past &
future

FALL

dead faces of tyranny
of hope   isms
form a history of
systems

torn apart in the flux of time

the limb
snaps

rotting in the long grass

DI

la so

chromatic

looking even now for
the rhymes the

connectives

DAC

some talk of
woman
man
the land &

bitten by the natural world
we disappear from
the decks of ships
the edge of
bridges
canoes
overturning in
northern lakes

gone

DOWN

in to
the natural world

beyond the city where the wild fields wait
the deer & foxes roam   beyond the grip of history
where our bodies decay
and war has not yet reached

this is what the land teaches

its presence

bitten

a desire to travel thru it

some books of journeying

a life

accounting for my presence

our presence in these times of war
times of peace

all times
ultimately passing

like this body

bitten

these bushes

animals or

TIC

BRIEFLY: The Birth/Death Cycle -- Hours 11, 12, 13 & 14
Hour 11:
1:35 to 2:35 a.m.

opening the present

farther & farther

that must be what's happening

father

noun
verb
other
myself

'i fathered you'

never thot it would be true

kept saying
'when Ellie became pregnant'
as tho it had nothing to do with me

author

a real issue here
'of creativity'

'have you seen the new issue?'

his penis his pen is
writ thru

'they gave each other a present'

i guess
time gives you
the past

'he's got a real past'
i.e. undesirable

'that's not a real present'
i.e. unsuitable

so who's coming
to dinner or anything

who came

well that's the issue

new nouns for
some old faces

me : father
Ellie : mother

& then --
history continues

little seed in time
flew out of me

little egg in
the great brine
right on time

con {
ception
crete
tent
densed
stancy

i.e. IN stant
IN fant

real 'ity'

ergo: thingness
finally linking in with
the great *we*

finally take our place in
the endless flow

birth means rebirth
means on you go on you goes
not 'ennui'
(a misreading) but
on *into* we

when the selves merge
a new self emerges

we
'three
we're not alone'

HOLD IT

'living in a memory'

'my how the time goes past'

months of it

i'll watch her change

'our' baby

its self

something inside of me
outside of me
inside of her
outside of her
(eventually)

'my echo
my shadow
& me'

'let's go out & find a present'
'that'd make a lovely present'
'may i ask who you're giving that present to'

indeed

in act

in perpetuity
of the race
never can escape the chase
of time of
the human fact of
the act

birth

but firth the burst
& then the first
born
bairn

no longer barren
(coz we was bare in
the bedroom)

Barrie's me &
Ellie's we &

makes three

'blue heaven'

's sake

they call them
'Pop' songs

any way you look at it
's the same
forwards & backwards
p o p

as in the motion
creates the notion
which arrives
is 'at'
& hence 'notation'
of the act or
fact of
the creation

but can i present the past? isn't the past always present? we don't live in the present or the past but the presently (i.e. theory of life as deferred potential (to a greater or lesser degree))

Interviewer:

So if sex is equated with writing...

Author:

Then birth would be publishing.

Interviewer:

Because its visible?

Author:

Because its a multiple.

(i can't remember the moment when it happened but it must have been in Vancouver. we figured that out for sure. conceiving where i was conceived. a second addition.)

'Poetic justice'

'his words ring true'

'a beautiful sentence'

POP ART

mother art too

craft

so you stand around & wait now
at the gateway to this world

THEY CAME FROM INNER SPACE

---

out of no where
out of here (he said gesturing)
into her
w---e___'___s born

(her
or he)
in the love roll
calls

'PRESENT!!'

Hour 12:
(unordered/incomplete)
11:00 to 11:53 a.m.

order

sweet seduction of that odour

shifts
            or is a door
            opens
            thru which the world
            's glimpsed
            tumbling

in form's a
space
            the door
defines
            (first)

                        & then this thing
moving
            we describe
relative to
                  the frame

                                    of reference

                                    up
side down

this

side down

               relative to   up

be
cause of
the machinery's delicacy &
balance (i'm) balance

'im or 'er

when the breath hhhhhs
leaves t'em

(shhhhh)

a sleep
& then
a wake

one take

a particular order in
a wall of doors

six walls of doors

hex
agon
y

a spell
a spill

<table>
<tr><td>as poll
as pull
as pall</td><td>}</td><td>i.e.</td><td>{</td><td>from the people
from the powerbrokers
from death</td></tr>
</table>

choices

the myriad voices of the worlds
the selves
shifting as the letters shift
'like' the letters

that's how we spell the world

conceptual alphabets

'look maw
i just made up a new word'

or-der

or dir-ect orders

or dor-ic columns

or dur-able things

or dar-ing thots

'i' makes up 'me'

M (l k j
[I] h g f)
E

first the nation
then the combination

politeraturecally
poethically

define the frame
defyin' the frame

or dar-ing
young man on
the fly-ing
tra-peze
-oid
fool
a loof

better use his
loaf

these definitions
things/themselves the
tarot has that ability
to rat
spills the beans on
our spells

unvoiced plans for the future

the past

order

or roads

stretch out from
this point
this centre
all around us
forever

like a dedication

for
ever

Hour 13:
6:35 to 7:35 a.m.

briefly

the heart does break

the aching muscle in the chest
carries more than the weight hangs from the body
from the barely perceiving brain
buried under the weight of loss

of grief

brief moment of clarity

stillborn

i never know him
never name him
bury him under the greening tree in the shadow of the old stone wall

falls away from me

into the earth at birth

unborn again

when our son died
i feared Ellie'd die too

a gnawing in the mind

blind terror

i held her all night
just to keep her to me

tho the heart pounds
the will shatters

you are broken

his spirit dead

our spirit

in this world

too quick

without explanation

gone

drove into the countryside
hours on the road to Point Pelee
south to the very bottom
skipped stones onto the lake
flick across the surface &

gone

into another world

like my sister Donna
dead at six weeks

or Ellie's brother Robert
dead at two years

into the slow dissolve of memory

a life

love's loss

passes

this grief

's past

in time

caring
awake all night &

past us

slipped thru the gap between the living & the dead

on

past this passing & this grief's hold

gone who was never ours to hold

past us

briefly

a life

time's alike

less thru loss

& yet

the loss at last passes too

of us

no 'baby makes three'

not ours

alive or dead

illusion of possession slips past us

GOD IT ALL SLIPS PAST US

so briefly

Hour 14:
1:35 to 2:35 a.m.

passages from death into life

'nothing but the river that flows'

not so much a line as a source

so that we move &
pass ages in the motion
foreward or
sideways or

time moves thru & around us

old father

old greybeard you touch us all

you are cliche & fate & fearful & sweet elixir

mostly you are there at the end of this sentence like a period.

except the period is what i just passed thru
or part of a general description this writing will come to fit

or except mostly i am always conscious of myself as older
never younger than
i am always looking backwards into the present
misreading
read the title as 'Hiding in the Unverse'
took it as true
found for myself

all these clouds

all this flickering air

all this breathing & blood flow & sometimes speech

some time's talk

this hour in the universe
oblivious
drunken voices in the street
1:45 a.m.
slam of car trunk &
vanishing clatter of motor

Glimpses of Vanished Originals

even Eden

'How should he know that peaks and valleys can so soon change?'

so

lost

in the one verse

never made it home

back

across that range & into that valley
dreamed so often as a child
the village at the end of the wild
beyond the hills & the sculpted park
whose streets i wandered
stores i browsed
books bought
awoke elated
two days later searching for them on my shelf &

nothing

only a void

touches you

briefly

eternal fascination

'when you're feeling blue'

from life thru life

'This minute sitting alone, page-boys all muted, I think of days of old: Hand in hand. Compose poems. Down twisting sidepaths towards limpid streams.'
-- Wang Wei, in a letter to P'ei Ti

'down into the world of men'

not so much a source but

crossing over

the trick is not to get your clothes wet

the trick is if you get your clothes wet to make it poetry

the trick is crossing over
not so much as belief but
as continuity

you do

tho greybeard kisses you
& you know you're not the first

he is horror & surrender & decay & translation

he is angel & spectre & griever & release

'i wish i'd never met you'
'if i never meet you again it'll be too soon'
'do drop in'
'why did i bother inviting you?'

not so much a continuity but a passage
from life to death or
unknown to unknown

parentheses

) life (

'stuck in the middle'
'torn in two'

'or three or four or more'

in some land
with me &

'If you say spring wind does not understand things
Why should it blow to us fallen flowers?'

never make it home

'never find the way back in a million years'

adrift in the void we cannot conceptualize
cannot grasp
rushing towards some unformulated nothingness
thru the dark & the dark the endless passages

Hour 15:
8:35 to 9:35 p.m.

1(2(conversations in another room

sound tracks

'can't leave them lying 'round'
'off the wall'
shuffle
over me
say hello to friends
CARRY ON (a conversation)

so maybe this is something like
starting over like
simileteneity

(this is just the babble before the music starts

this is just the start)

being & begin
the chicken & the egg &
the gee makes the horse giddy
(waves waver
all-a-quaver
quivering art he start with) UP definite rhythm
deaf night noise
(silence in the midst of
these human conditions)

meditation
(head on)

building the composition

'i could hear you singing
after all there's noone there'

HERE (guitar)

'i know it yeah
underneath the particles'

ART (piano)

'figuring out's
flying on the fingers take you'

IN (bass)

'the yeah that talk
not to take time tightly'

NO (drums)

JUST FRIENDS!!

all around me
so that i wanted to say
'i'm trying to write'
1/2/3/4
i'm tying the right words together

counter-rhythms
a weight a history is
figures
an improvisation

saints & angels
giants, gods &

going for the moment

gone

an improve situation you
'go for broke'
'flat out'
away
like a horse called SHIP OF STATE
the trick's to finish in the money honey
do you like a muddy track?
all that indefinite future
wavering between you &
the finish line

a fine line

that line of the poem you just wrote
torn by conflicting emotions

'you don't love me
like i love you'

of course not

ill logic

'nobody could'

the difference between two heads starts with a single thot

certain stupid arguments
Ellie & me fighting over whether the room was too hot
forgetting metabolic differences
all these conversations in the same room
the head buzzes
you almost answer
could shout yourself hoarse in
this notion of noise

a night out

of sync
of rhythm
of the life of friends &

social graces

moments with the muse's heirs

not solo
tho the solo's taken

in the end
where does the poem live but in this din
in the midst of this accompaniment
so much a part of the intent
its written out of
audio densities i return it to)3)4

Hour 16:
3:35 to 4:35 p.m.

What did i see in the night?

What vision?

What images of war & death?

That there are millions who die
violently
that we are used to it
at a distance
numbed
not quite indifferent
we add our voices to the chorus
muted
unable to believe the tales of torture &
brutaliy
speak nonetheless
out of puzzlement
perceived horror
these endless chronicles of
genocide
what seems often the suicidal impulse to
protest
from moral outrage
from grief
from the felt inequity & inhumanity
of which the sum's a helpless feeling in the chest
beats at you
claws at the eyes
the tongue
all yearning to turn inward & be mute
blind
some kind of vision of gentleness
a strange peace
in which the beast in us is stilled
the greed, the bloodlust & the envy willed to sleep
but it exists.

What did i see in the night?

Was it more than this?

That we are lulled not by what is best in us
but by the petty differences
                                        hurt by slights
a tone of voice
                        the noise of our simple jealousies
blocks out the screaming of the world
blurs the overwhelming helplessness

We keep the stage small on which we strut
& claim as epic the very ordinariness
of our experience
                          shield within our lives
the same murderous emotions we deplore
there is nowhere we turn that is not so.

Even poetry has its posturing superiority.

What did I see in the night?

                                          My own face in the mirror
my eyes
                behind which terror of such violence hides
so that I turn away too often
overwhelmed
                      from the news
6000 disappeared in Argentina
the systematic killings in Cambodia
these ills & worse of the world
what am i to do with
the ineffectiveness of the poem
that it reaches only the converted
only those to whom such messages get thru
that it is not a gun
nor a means to peace
but only that least of things
words
              but that they mean so much to me
& that i see the world most clearly
                                                thru them.

What did i see in the mirror but something human
ruled by its own fears & dreams
that clings to its mate in the darkness weeping
frightened of death & its own mortality
the uncertainty of its future.

What did i see in the night but this
the great void of human history
a vision of the false mystery our lives assume
because we crowd these rooms with insignificances
beyond which i heard a screaming & a singing
& there is such desperation in me
to hear it so clearly
i will never forget it

that noise /
/ that tune

Hour 17:
5:35 to 6:35 p.m.

two freighters gliding in the distance
as if they would finally meet & touch
somewhere south of here
in the grey blue haze of Lake Erie
the different planes & surfaces become unclear
collision course

feet in the crashing waves at Pelee's tip
sun in a haze above me
hugeness of the sky surrounds this i
the mind beats against the skin contains this brain
& only that shell of flesh & bone remains
maintains this sundering

empty it out

empty it out

only the wind moving in the tear ducts
blowing into my open mouth
my throat carries this noise & force within
it is consumed
blood thrives on it
all thot this animal flesh contains
thrives on it

gulls in clouds above & around
Pelee Island's outline over the waves
so little to say when the birds scream & the wind
the world is in voice around me

all of this
the personal references
the names
nothing more than shrill chatter
noise
reaching some day a final destination
unintelligible vocabulary
history

earlier today
Ellie & i at Southwold earthworks
pacing the perimeter
(Arthur's Table? Mayborough?)
no trace of a maker remains
these monuments we raise, books we write,
wind up in a lost tongue
finally all reference vanishes

tho reason points out the folly
a voice is born again

tho the different purposes & meanings remain unclear
this voice is born again

empty it out

empty it out

i have this dumb shout within me
a lifetime cannot approximate

i have this wish to write the world i can never realize

stand here   mouth open

air fills me

blown away

in the day to day hugeness of this hazy being
i can never take it all in

i have this sentence i must finish

i have this poem i must write

the boats steam away
west towards Lake Huron
east to Lake Ontario
the planes & surfaces foreshorten & change

bird song & wave noise

wind & whistling air

in the midst of
there is something

a presence or a silence
an absence or the pressure of

(leaving Southwold
drove west
paused near Morpeth where Lampman's buried
read his lines inscribed in the graveyard:

'Yet, patience -- there shall come
Many great voices from life's outer sea,
Hours of strange triumph, and when few men heed,
Murmurs and glimpses of eternity.')

THERE

Hour 18:
12:35 to 1:35 a.m.

three months of lines recurring in the mind

driving south from North Bay
1 a.m. August 10th 1981
full moon scudding from behind dark clouds
thot 'this is where the poem begins'

or later
Ellie in labour (September 16th)
the notion of poetry works at the back of the brain
no matter the hour of the day or night
no matter the hour come to in a life
finally the stuff of which the poem is made
our infant daughter Sarah in my arms
'is this where the poem begins?

double reverses

sey yes i sey yes

12:45 a.m.
an evening spent with friends --
bissett, Arlene Lampert, Janine & Robert Zend
-- that list enters the writing again
like a leaf picked up on the shoe & tracked in
the details of my life dragged into the poem
in part at least
immaterial as the leaf
as any life
as the fleeting impressions of this cold October night

car slam

background hum of furnace & fridge

on the edge of being on edge

Sarah's born
ten weeks before her time
searching for a line of entry

'i didn't have the time'
'not enough hours in the day'
'where has the time gone to'

drive around three months
waiting for myself to makes the move
too full of feeling to articulate it

driving south on Hwy 11
the moon filled the windshield of the car
& the stars, when the clouds cleared,
i almost lost my way driving into them

like later
panicked
driving south into Toronto
late call to say
'your baby's being born'
useless with too fast emotion
what was to stop me from driving into the lake
except that edge of consciousness we cling to
like a road, a breakwater, or
the memory of a mapped route home

the moon fills my mind
dropped into the poem
kicking & screaming
weeks in the premature nurseries
Ellie watching baby after baby, newborn,
rushed into incubators, under sunlamps,
heels pricked for blood, lungs suctioned of fluid,
faces turning blue from cyanosis,
bradycardia, apnea,
a life, some lives, begin

driving south
too tired to drive anymore
sleep four hours then hit the road
again
smashed down onto that line of thot
a limitation
we bump up against the world
the day to day waver of a continent
smashed into by waves &
eaten away

telling our daughter
all she has to do is
gain a little weight (every day)
Ellie pumping her breasts for milk
eatin' away

the moon fragments
broken by invisible clouds
press round it like
similes & metaphors the moon evokes

writing south
too tired to write anymore
October 30th 1981
sleep four hours
drive out to Simcoe
read again

poems

like this one

leaves from a book
tracked into your life Sarah
clinging to me

'is this where the poem begins?'

sey yes i sey yes
i sey yes i
sey yes

Hour 19:
9:35 to 10:35 p.m.
(for Ellie)

heartbeat
heartbeat
heartbeat
heartbeat
heartbeat
heartbeat
heartbeat   of the heart dear hart
heartbeat
heartbeat   hairtō day &
heartbeat   cor
heartbeat   tomorrow
heartbeat
heartbeat
heartbeat
heartbeat
heartbeat   of intellect
heartbeat   (memory)
heartbeat   (   )
heartbeat
heartbeat
heartbeat
heartbeat   heart of grace
heartbeat   hart of grease
heartbeat   herte of gresse
heartbeat
heartbeat
heartbeat   stout heart
heartbeat   'as one doth that taketh a sodyne courage'
heartbeat   cordage
heartbeat
heartbeat
heartbeat   'Heart of oaks are our ships,
heartbeat   heart of oak are our men'
heartbeat   women
heartbeat
heartbeat
heartbeat
heartbeat
heartbeat   of affection of

heartbeat
heartbeat
heartbeat
heartbeat
heartbeat recordrecorder
heartbeat
heartbeat heart or
heartbeat mind
heartbeat
heartbeat
heartbeat 'That dwelled in his hertë
heartbeat sike and sore,
heartbeat Gan faillen when the hertë
heartbeat feltë deth;'
heartbeat
heartbeat
heartbeat heart-burning
heartbeat heart-blood
heartbeat heart-breaking
heartbeat heart-ache
heartbeat
heartbeat
heartbeat 'all that human hearts endure'
heartbeat
heartbeat
heartbeat heart-less
heartbeat heart-ease
heartbeat heart-felt
heartbeat heart-whole
heartbeat
heartbeat
heartbeat heart-sick
heartbeat
heartbeat
heartbeat
heartbeat 'a change of heart'
heartbeat ('in the heart or in the head?')
heartbeat
heartbeat
heartbeat
heartbeat 'hearts are in the right place'
heartbeat whence hearty,
heartbeat heartily,
heartbeat hearten
heartbeat
heartbeat

heartbeat
heartbeat 'you gotta have...'
heartbeat it
heartbeat
heartbeat
heartbeat 'Vpon the knees of our hearts
heartbeat to agonize
heartbeat our most constant
heartbeat faith'
heartbeat
heartbeat
heartbeat whence 'miles & miles & miles of heart'
heartbeat
heartbeat
heartbeat
heartbeat 'Behould the ears of my hart,
heartbeat are set before thee,'
heartbeat
heartbeat
heartbeat 'My wife & I fell out a little...
heartbeat she cried, poor heart!
heartbeat which I was troubled for'
heartbeat
heartbeat
heartbeat
heartbeat 'all you really need is...'
heartbeat
heartbeat
heartbeat
heartbeat
heartbeat
heartbeat
heartbeat

heartbeat
heartbeat
heartbeat
heartbeat
heartbeat
heartbeat
heartbeat
heartbeat
heartbeat
heartbeat
heartbeat divided heart
heartbeat

heartbeat
heartbeat
heartbeat
heartbeat
heartbeat
heartbeat
heartbeat
heartbeat
heartbeat
heartbeat
heartbeat
heartbeat
heartbeat
heartbeat
heartbeat
heartbeat
heartbeat
heartbeat
heartbeat
heartbeat
heartbeat
heartbeat
heartbeat
heartbeat
heartbeat
heartbeat
heartbeat
heartbeat
heartbeat
heartbeat
heartbeat
heartbeat
heartbeat
heartbeat
heartbeat
heartbeat
heartbeat
heartbeat
heartbeat
heartbeat
heartbeat
heartbeat
heartbeat
heartbeat
heartbeat

heart of
darkness

or:

to be at
the heart of things

to have
a heart to
heart

hear a
hear b
hear c
heard

hear e
hear f
hear g

hear h
hear i
hear j
heark

hear l
hear m
hear n
hear o
hear p

hear q
hear r
hears
heart

hear u
hear v

hear w
hear x

hear y
hear z

heartbeat
heartbeat
heartbeat
heartbeat
heartbeat 'Once upon a time
heartbeat My heart was just an organ,'
heartbeat -- Rodgers & Hart
heartbeat
heartbeat
heartbeat
heartbeat in the heart of the thicket
heartbeat in the heart of the fire
heartbeat in the heart of the city
heartbeat in the heart of the night
heartbeat
heartbeat
heartbeat
heartbeat
heartbeat
heartbeat (in the heat of the moment i gave you my heart)
heartbeat
heartbeat
heartbeat
heartbeat
heartbeat
heartbeat 'Now we're getting to the heart of it!'
heartbeat sweetheart
heartbeat
heartbeat
heartbeat
heartbeat
heartbeat
heartbeat
heartbeat
heartbeat
heartbeat
heartbeat
heartbeat
heartbeat
heartbeat
heartbeat
heartbeat
heartbeat
heartbeat
heartbeat

THE GRAMMAR TRILOGY -- Hours 20, 21 & 22
Hour 20:
12:35 to 1:35 a.m.

bio
geo } graphy

writing a self
a country

landscape a can be in

clOud
cl_ud

(or, as in that poem i never published
(not knowing the etymology):

CLOUD
O
O
O
STONE

too much the clod to see it then
(ear to the earth))

grammar, grandma. now
in your 97th year
you've outlived most of them
-- a husband
-- two daughters
-- a son
-- only my mother & your other son left
the rest of us
grandchildren, great & great great grandchildren,
you feel further & further away from
we become less real
the longer your life becomes

family

bio } logos
geo }

tonight
misreading my notes
mistake the time
miswrite this hour

lo { gos
lo { cal

miss writing?

con { fusion
con { nection

I { con { O { graphy

IO (inventor of the 5 vowels)
sister of Phoroneus
(variously Bran, Barn, Brennus, etc.
reincarnated as a crow)

(all this out of the <u>con</u> <u>graphy</u>
(the fusion which is the nection) the
<u>bio</u> <u>geo</u>)

we
of grandma, ma,
me & Sarah

<u>beING</u>
INGwe

(founder of the English tribes
inventor of the runic alphabet)

the continuous presence
the contiguous present

ethereal earth eel

out of rhythm
pattern

CON { fusion
nection

(a gain)

AM BIG!
u ity?

i-i-i-i
/ o my sombre era o

(line thru history)

bi
etym
gene
martyr
ge
} OLOGY

or all a G
(which is my birth'd A
September 30th being G's beginning
11th month in the Bethluisnion

grammar
:the relations of words in
a sentence

she is my grammar
her name is Agnes

sent m's
sent n's

m art
yr all a G

what i thot was endin/g
beginin/g
writin/g

in g we

Hour 21:
11:25 p.m. to 12:40 a.m.

8:45 p.m.
Bob phoned to say
'grandma's dead'

'that minute seemed like an hour'
subjective subject
i've covered the ground before

ground grandma
you were the gave in my give
a love of women
flows from what you taught me
of them

of you

of the two of us
& how we met

you taught me games
made up rules
changed them to your purposes

grandma Nichol
the year she died
talked constantly of heaven
sang hymns
some afterlife a vision

you never mentioned heaven once
just earth
& Walter Workman
whom you'd married
who i resemble
& Plunkett, Saskatchewan,
children you birthed
encouraged to write your story
that story's over
which is why this poem begins

'The horses were out in the fields you see, the river ran all through that patch, & this horse, that was old Muse, she was reaching up for some leaves on the tree that was standing on the bank & it broke, & this great big turtle, there must have been a turtle right there, slid out from under...'

turtle (that link with age)
muse (a horse here (in disguise))
i heard such tales from you myths
you were my dumb gazing at night skies
world before my birth read for signs
inhabited the wild west my father dreams of

it was all local reference your life
Walter dying
you were 57
worked then as a housekeeper til age 72
work was the thing made sense to you

'When I was 10 or 11 a neighbour lady wanted me to come & look after her 3 children while she did some housecleaning. Well this place was only a mile and a half from home. I could look over & see the rest of the kids playing around the yard, which made me homesick. I stayed 3 days & then went home. She gave me 3 yds of calico which was then about 8 cents a yard. It was red with a very small white dot. I thot a lot of that dress. I guess because I had made it myself.'

'Memories of Agnes Leigh Workman, born October 8th, 1885, the story of my life, as I can remember, I'm becoming quite forgetful. This is supposed to be as far back as I can remember. I think I was 4 years old at the time. This is in South Dakota & we'd been living on a 40 acre farm. That was what a man was allowed to take as a homestead, & my dad wanted to get to where he could have more land to farm so we were moving to this other place that had some cattle & dad was driving a wagon that was loaded with our household goods, which I don't think was very much, & my mother was driving this old horse named Tom hitched to this buggy, 3 or 4 of us kids were in the buggy, & Dell fell out. She was about 2 years old. She fell between the front wheel & the side of the buggy. The old horse stopped dead still & didn't move until Ma got back in the buggy with Dell. She wasn't hurt.'

miracles
   or so they seemed
miraculous world of memory
dusty hotels & vanished dirt streets
Plunkett as a name in Heaven

you are gone now
into the <u>or</u>
remembrance's revision
this side the flesh
weeping because we miss you
only the mind retains
again
   memory fragments
   flickers &

'Then I remember another time, I guess that same fall when I was 4, they had the cows in the corral at the back of the barn where my mother & dad were milking. I took my tin cup & went out where they were to get the cup filled & one of the cows picked me up between her horns & was carrying me around.' &

 birth

    death

       Agnes

           wife
           lover
             mother
           grandmother

recalling the fall Warren Tallman & i visited you
you put on the trick nose   the trick feet
stood there   leaning on your cane   laughing

you knew the ridiculousness of it all

falls away

& i miss you
love you
your quick twist of wit

twists inside me

life

loved you
love you

this

Hour 22:
12:35 to 1:35 p.m.

death you enter the poem as you always do
-- disruptor

whatever the order or structure
we must reckon you in
a sum
cuts across
some vision of perfection we cling to

corruptor of our flesh
decay
        ec(ho) in our day leading
this art's d(ec(co))ay?
oration contains its fallibility
humanity's struck sure
brief span of which we write & writ
your dark unknowing surrounds it

decORATION
ARTifice

(it melts in
the heat of
the emotions)

this punning un's me
o pun's a door in
the floor i
fall thru
surface after surface

de)a(th
de)c(ay
de)p(th

i am shopping between th a & p
slips ship me
sea to middle c
a full chord or dischord
mu si c
or say sea
bond
    a band on ship
in St Rument's litany

you are the siren on the rock c's road
calling

gazing out the window on a 26th floor
this fear of falling's
tempt } ation
or } ation

c creates an action

a life wavers

death you are the embodiment of contradiction
the fixer
finalizer gives us illusions of control
because of the limits you impose

hours shift
illusionary 'our'

'at a time like this'
's all time mate
(what the d ate was ours)

'im's mortal
'er's mortal

hopin's adored in
the floor i
fall thru
nothing to cling to but
the puncertainty
you unme death   into the punbelieveable void
where nothing i have clung to clings

i sing anyway

of mortality

of the death of family

pun
a } ctual

she slipped away in her sleep'
'she's gone'

old English verb from which 'dead' came
thru which 'death' entered the language
lost

we are slipping after you
verb
'part of speech which signifies
to be, to do or
to suffer'
we are chasing you into the mystery of after
lost verb
lost life

our are hour makes the phase phrase
sparse shares the origin of speech

we are sprinkled or scattered

mere babellers

sum }
for } mer

random/accident/collison/mutation

the births
the deaths

poetry

Hour 23:
6:35 to 7:35 p.m.
(in memory of Visvaldis Upenieks)

chemical change — Jim Brown

If I beat it,
am I making music? — R. Murray Schafer

th' Passion Lilies cry out to him — Joe Rosenblatt
'HURRY
HURRY
(
listen i shudda got rid of yu a long — bill bissett
time ago
)
LISTEN GEORGE IT'S JAZZ AND POETRY TOO IT'S A NO-MIND — Lionel Kearns
instantaneous being with it through go you step
out on the ice a hulking mass of reflex energy
all his settings — sean o'huigin
ready for the
letting loose of
batterings of
sound across
the bridge to
man.

the trouble was i realized — Earle Birney
just before i started howling
somebody had been watching all along
not knoing not knoing — David UU
what what
had been had been
written
and sed
resound

or that the time pass
the sound
gone
grounded the speech
the body of grammar
gone beyond the reach of real hearing
only the reel left
unwinding

Silent is my chapel; silent is my holy place;
Over my house, my gate, and my fields
silence is poured out.

Lamentation for
Ishtar

inspiration
as it leaves the body
incidental
          death is
and makes of any work
a book of
the dead   structures
we establish   arbitrary

who have listened much
yet not recognized; and
who, though recognizing, are, nevertheless
weak in familiarity.

The Tibetan Book
of the Dead

in the space of
a month
          a heartbeat
friends fall
out of your life
        your heart
     of suffering

I have to expect,
O my lady, judgement of confusion &
violence. Death & trouble are
bringing me to an end --

Lamentation for
Ishtar

lives we had built together
fade, will fade, change, die
visions, reel, i
zations of
the voice
trapped in
the magnetic pull of

reel{ ing / ation } / no

tation, these forms   arguments for the voice
that frail choice

gone soon into great noise
silence marks an end to our speech
choices each of us made
to be heard
caught then
in the endless re-vision of
the oral

th full breath — bill bissett
is what knowledge is, is human, is
wholly real, includes what is
in all things

Rhythm says: 'I am here and — R. Murray Schafer
I want to go there;
all that debris arms & legs & hair — Jim Brown
bruised purple blossom along white
flushing skin

(there's no — sean o'huigin
rection
any more.)

endless poem — Lionel Kearns

draw th' tongue in — Joe Rosenblatt
draw th' tongue out

walk alone in the wind and the dusk — Earle Birney
toward the beautiful antediluvian sky

a breath — David UU
taken . your
name in our
words . a
desire for
presence

the sound of you Mother/Father
echoes
flickering
a world

Hour 24:
11:35 a.m. to 12:35 p.m.

'I awoke as if from sleep,
a new light broke on me'

musics

or that there are songs in
the head   spheres
in which the brain moves
harmonies
dischords
a turn

fixed instance of the flux

or the brain
blanking, eyes lidding
closing down
into
a netherworld

where gods walk
saints talk to us, Jove
the alchemical tin
'Joseph he was an tin man'
oversaw the alchemical change of Christ
translation into the afterlife
a world

as heaven was
the heavens, Kepler saw
a sphere where sun was God
Jesus the fixed stars
Holy Ghost between

we aim now for galactic centre or
beyond that another
round which galaxies spin
spun out on the rim of the Milky Way
further & further from where we are
is where knowledge leads us

the rain forests of Venus
man-made canals of Mars
gone now   these celestial mechanics
tinker with our knowledge of our self
sure centre of a universe
made smaller, less significant daily,
all knowledge finally a lesson in humility

synchronicity

metaphor

discarded models of the universe
the mind

atomic world of tiny solar systems

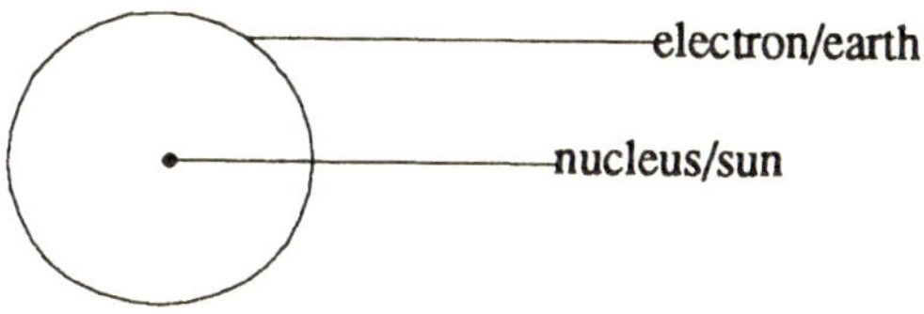

i lived on one once
somewhere in a nanomoment in the mind
saw the face of God
neutrons & protons in constant conflict
split
        'brighter than a thousand suns'
& then
the horror of it over & over

knowledge strips the self away, the flesh
shifting faces of a world
we cannot pretend to grasp
Babel takes new forms & figures
we point our towers heavenward
relocate belief
                    blow God's old homes apart
our lives split
                    families
reinvoke the old forms   desperately
but nothing holds

it is all vanity   arrogance
we are lead further out   or further in

                              mercurial 

                              hunger
                              the only constant in
                              this brief history of
                              our kind
our songs fleeting, temporal,
against these larger musics
we glimpse notation of
but never hear

Hour 25:
2:35 to 3:35 a.m.

'somewhere there's music'

how faint, the tune
falls over & over
the ear drums echo
stirrup, chirrup
(a cricket somewhere in the room

there's music

or) there
pressure of air on the still moving face
shift in the drift that age presses on the body
vocalabulary

the way that word 'drift' keeps drifting in
from what origin? continental or wood or snow or
'i get your drift'
right in the face
the poem snowballs
voKABALLAry

'Dr. if this is the cure
what's the sickness?'

dis-ease

(a state that thinking is)

'don't think such bad thots'
'it's not such a bad idea'
'he's so lost in thot he can't hear us'

adrift or

one drift or

'wonder if
they really get my drift'

could, be

'all the conditional conditions that may, be'
MURPHY'S LAW (circa 1983), & hence
'somewhere there's heaven' even

'tell me your idea'

'show me your I.D.'

or like my sister Dea said

, age three,
'I Dea'
& pointed to herself

(Heisenberg's principle of one certainty
falls over & over on
the ear drummmmmmmmm

a-tom-tom-tom-tom-tom-ic age
& now the atom is passé
(discarded model, like a Model A)

'atomic age' evokes the 1950's

we're Model A/T's now
all hydrogen & heavy water &

'I'm gonna take you on a sea cruise'
miss-a-lot
if you don't watch out

the window
narrows

'how high the moon')

pressure of air on a still moving face

age presses on the body

'im presses

presses it out

Hour 26:
5:35 to 6:35 a.m.
(for Ellie -- a valentine)

E akahele i ka mamo a I,
o kolo mai ka mole uaua.

Beware the descendants of I,
lest the tough roots crawl forth.

Hawaiian Proverb
translated by Mary Kawena Pukui

nothing to consider   but love
the heart   how words & the blood
flow
          stirred
by the thot of her
the flesh of her
her

        in the shadowed dark
leeward of the Koolau Range
stars invisible above the clouds
spread out over these mountains
this valley
                    in the heat of the pre-dawn
the mind is not
is blank
             except for the automatic gesture of
of longing
runs on beyond the necessary body of desire
like the whirring fan in
this tiny room
stirs the thot the
fabric of
the curtain

so little to say
when it is the body desired
the words
                not part of that urge
speech denoting separation
'i' has to talk to 'you'
because the one wants the two
gether

in the hush of love
with only the flesh between
the pure murmur that is meaning merges
the tongue   silenced
in the shadowed valleys
among the limbs
                              the branchings of
longing   eased   erased
all trace of language gone

speech of us
we carry that 'each' there
on the tongue   in the concept
'reach-out-to-you'
across these distances
flesh creates

the cells are just that

until we touch

so little between us
& yet
        so much

Honolulu
February 14th 1984

MIDDLE INITIAL SEQUEL
Hour 27:
3:35 to 4:35 a.m.

Hallowed evening's eve

dying day's light's beginning

first hours of dawn
the spirit sways
back & forth within this frail shell
shuck the p
i am again
b n
    middle initial i am born into
'm no p but
initially b
chance letter of creation
the arbitrariness of sighin's names

all hallowed eve
she took the ribbing
a damned evening of spooks
ghosts
muse-eum source-ery
witch'll it be
p n o playing
middle c initial
keys   a scale
of values
al vues of
the arbored rare eve ness of
signs

wit, Tiw,
in the still dark hour of your name day
i name too
one of the old gods the ceremony lost reference to
see how the banned play on
c { luster of notes
  { hords

tiwns
melodeus we never lose   the thread of
walking the dark streets in the hours before dawn
spikes of frost clustering 'round the street lamps
the threat of
snow   the given
descends all around us &
the ungiven
the seen

act one
two
three

intials
here please

because i have made a change
desire you witness it

hear please

the changes the fingers play
the fingers the changes play
changes the fingers play the
fingers the changes play the
play changes the fingers the
changes play the fingers the
fingers play the changes the
play fingers the changes the
first middle last initial
crone logical eve witch
dei ends begins day

Tuesday, October 30th, 1984

in place of Hour 28
1:30 a.m. to 1:59 a.m.

words, finally, for anyone who wants them

in the midst of the great silence which surrounds
in the midst of this instance of the noise

because there is not order in the world

because there is more madness than any one of us can deal with
more tragedy
                        the deaths, daily,
nothing new in news
                                only the endless cycle
bright blade of history cutting into itself

because there are words & more words
uncounted books deploring our inhumanity
prizes for those who merely spoke from conscience
a competition & a judging

because there is now the tyranny of quantity
the sheer mass of literature
that concept becoming clear
the old notion of immortality seen for what it is
a preening in the bleak light history reflects
 -- READ ME -- READ ME --
                                                the weight of words shifts

---

(in the library stacks the shelves grow fuller, the buildings forced to expand, the budgets cut, nonexistant, of course the voices become more muted, even tho they are screaming, even tho they have things to say, things that you might want to hear, the words disappear into the dust, the darkness, the books closed and noone here to read them, noone here to take them from the shelves, anything any one of us might say becoming simply what it is, ink on yellowing pages, disappearing into this wait of words, the unvoiced endless hours)

Book III

CONTINENTAL TRANCE

'We cannot retrace our steps, going forward may be the same as going backwards. We cannot retrace our steps, retrace our steps. All my long life, all my life, we do not retrace our steps, all my long life, but.'

Gertrude Stein
The Mother Of Us All

minus the ALL ABOARD

minus my father waving

minus the CN logo

minus my mother waving

minus seventeen years of my life
Ellie & me
our unborn child in her belly
heading east
out of Vancouver
July 27th
8 p.m.
nineteen eighty-
1.

*

what i wanted to write:
'this is how it begins' or
'pulling into New Westminster'

what actually happened:
took a different route
skipped the canneries of New Westminster entirely

(so much for nostalgia or
plotting the poem in advance)

walking up to the snack bar
seven cars to the front
the sleeping car porter three cars ahead
making the beds
the teenage kid said to him
(admiringly) 'you've got it all worked out eh'
as he flipped the mattress down
upper to lower
berth
  & the porter said
'if i had it all worked out
i wouldn't be doing this'

*

crossing the Fraser River
Port Mann in the night
lights out the left window of
the train

darker outline of the mountains
dark blue of the sky
minus the stars
out this left window on the universe

*

the old guy who spoke to the porter just now said:
'my wife wanted to take this trip
before she takes her heavenly trip'

my grandma, 96, earlier today said:
'i don't think i wanta stay around too many more'

Ellie's sitting across from me
reading Peter Dickinson's *One Foot In The Grave*
& in the first draft of this poem i wrote:
'minus these coincidences
what is the world trying to tell me?'

minus -- the word returns
-- some notion of absence (not a life)
subtracting the miles travelled east
(minus mine -- us)
loosing all notion of possession
aboard this mixed metaphor

*

upper berth swaying in the darkness
click as the wheels clack off the miles

two women pass thru
drunk from the observation car
the one talking at the top of her voice
i say 'shut up' loudly

the woman shuts up
& her friend
lowering her voice whispers back
'fuck off'

lullabies in the real world

*

insistent instances

Kamloops in the early morning

someone, going crazy in their roomette,
rings the porter's bell repeatedly

seven a.m.

no way to sleep again

stagger forward to breakfast
the eggs taste of plastic or pam

drink tea
lurch up to the observation car
watch the mountains loom by

back in the sleeper car
one porter scratches the other porter's knees
'stop it! you know what that does to me!'

Blue River at ten
my cousin Donna's nursing station visible thru the trees

you too, Nicky,
none of us escapes these details
presences
even in these wilds
rocking back & forth
eastward on this western train

*

beginnings & endings

discrete frames in
a continuous flow

the japanese family talking
words i don't know

a horse glimpsed from the window
a man at the river's side
things i have knowledge of but cannot account for

like the flowers i saw
earlier today
purple spikes driven up
interspersed among the charred stumps of the fired forest

or the mountain's high green meadow
visible above the clouds

or the brook the train crossed even as i wrote these words
rushing down
carrying its content
into the larger lakes & rivers of the world

*

'because i was raised on trains'
-- this is the line that kept recurring to me
all night

'because i criss-crossed the west with
my mother & father'
-- the only other line i could find to write
remembering
as the woman across from us slaps her son's fingers
spilling the peanuts my father bought
all down the aisle of the train, 1954,
or dad yelling at me, 1948,
because i was running back & forth to the water cooler,
the newsy's face that same trip,
pissed off at his job,
twisted in a grimace i was intended to read as genial

random information intrudes each time i ride these rails
maybe for the last time
headline in that Vancouver paper
GOVERNMENT AXES TRANS-CONTINENTAL LINE THRU JASPER
part of my memory disappears
1500 jobs & a slice of history

'because i criss-crossed the west with
my mother & father'

'because i was raised on trains'

*

the conductor takes our luncheon reservations
'1:15'

but at five to 1 says 'its five to 2 --
set your watch ahead'

nothing's fixed aboard this paradox
affects more than we believe

flux logic

we eat at 2:15

*

ten minutes outside of Jasper
the line between sadism & masochism is drawn

as his one year old son hits his other son with a wire brush
the father across from us says to him:
'hit yourself with it!'

masochism wins --
the kid starts hitting himself
at least once for every time he hits his brother

WHACK   WHACK

following this tack
hitting the track to town

*

'too much like a rock song'
-- what i thot as i ended the previous poem

how come that voice keeps butting in?

why the need to resolve parameters?

why not the rush of
the asymetrical
arhythmic
world?

why not the y <u>not</u> the z
in the unwritten alphabets ahead?

*

okay we'll start there
with st utter's subtler statement

when the riddle's rid of rid
dle remains
ashine with its own kind of mystery

half words
half visions

the train pulls out of Jasper
three hours late

is this the st ate of my mind
or does that saint exist
beyond these twisting tracks
this train of thot?

*

so there it is

the literal metaphor or symbol

linear narrative of random sequential thots

accidents of geography, history & circumstance

the given

*

i don't like the 'symbol'
except as accent to the basic drum
of consciousness

i don't like the 'like'
except as entrance to
a "pataphysical reality

i like the play of words
of life   the moment when the feelings focus
    absolutely   a description

which is what st ate meant?   yes
my st ate meant
this

*

whistle

pulling over the level crossings
in the gathering dark into Edmonton

drainage ditches gleaming in the last light
clusters of buildings & trees

as night falls the sky reverses
dark clouds against a lighter blue

& the mind reverses
sleep takes
loosing the dream you

*

two hours from Saskatoon
fingernail of moon in the eastern sky
the pastel gray clouds at dawn
blow over the pinkening horizon
train gathering speed all the while
the berth shakes back & forth &
forth over the prairie

the revelation is in the blue dome of air
beneath which this train & the dawn appear
blue as the robin's egg i found age two
shattered on the sidewalk
bits of curved blue flung all about
& the train of thot it lead to

blue as that imagined sky that day
when the clouds were white
& the prairies lay over the mountains
in my future

*

mist of rain across the far horizon

heading out of Saskatoon
6:35 a.m. July 31st
the sky is a constant gray
& the fields of wheat, alfalfa, clover, grass, etc.
stretch away for miles in all directions

encompassed we make our way
thru the middle of Canada
east towards Winnipeg

the mid-summer morning rain

these middle days

*

later
a cultivator
then an elevator

somewhere between Nokomis & Raymore
(Semans to be exact)
two perfect stone circles
in a playground beside the tracks
except the circles are made of old tractor tires
(i can see this as we draw closer)

like that day
looking for the stones of Shap
saw a perfect circle beyond the crest of the next hill
lost sight of as we raced down into the valley, thrilled,
up & over, it was gone,
only a raggedy row of sheep in that field beyond

this is how the world is
rimes that disappear as you draw closer to their sense
dense clumps of trees
scattered across the open fields
notation
in the landscape of a nation &
a revelation

*

vanishing

down into the valley
tracking a forgotten river bottom
thru the farms, the ordered fences,
this old order is all around us
as we cross the border into Manitoba

saints you are gone
part of an older order of this poem
as Brun, too, is gone, sleeps with the other giants of his race
presences you can trace in Lampman, Roberts, et al
nineteenth century notions of this place

my unborn child
will never cover these miles we cover in this way

of life
vanishing

nothing visible no

a vast shining

*

the field of sunflowers stretches to the horizon
under this july sun
the clouds are isolate
mirror the disparate clumps of trees
& the fields & sky weave thru & around them
rime in the clear blue sloughs & streams

we move as in a dream
the mothers down the aisle screaming at their children
the guy across from me whistling the Colonel Bogey March

it will make sense yet
this blue & green
these fragmentary lives & conversations
& the white world, saints' home, in between

*

two hour delay in the Winnipeg station
'they're looking for an engine for the train'

the things that get displaced are major
they leave you stranded tho you know your destination

'i'm getting out of here'

sometimes there's no getting
aboard a-
way
            even if your ticket's punched

*

okay saints
i hear you babbling
press your way with your complaints into this scenery

someone spoke of you
as tho you were a literary device
more a vice i keep returning to

tho the order here's another one
your faces rise above these tree lines
there's a conversation we all come back to

so many years spent talking with you
a willed hallucination
more than continental
a kind of lifelong trance

& these pauses
on these sidings
waiting for that load of freight to pass

*

beside the track

drowned trees
water lilies

fish break
the surface of the lake

as i look back

*

'where is this poem going?'
'Toronto'

'what does it teach us?'
'how coincidence reaches into our lives &
instructs us'

the 19th century knew
any narrative, like life,
is where coincidence leads you

given, of course, the conscious choice of voice
the train of thot you choose

*

this next bit doesn't quite cohere

already past tense
or converted to a noun
when its the bite of consciousness eludes you

the flickering light thru the trees
sets up an echo in my brain
petit mal
makes me want to puke

but the trees
so clustered
a bird could walk the branches
a thousand miles or more

it is a map of consciousness
what the light yields disgorges
perceived thru a pattern of branches
the birds fly free of

*

in Hornpaye
the sign on the building i could see from the road read 'OTHING'
i reconstructed as 'NOTHING'
because it looked like it was falling down
as Ellie & i drew closer
i read, suddenly, as 'CLOTHING'
windows boarded up & broken

like my life-long wish
that i might clothe myself finally in belief
& realize:

> the name of death is 'NOTHING'
> the name of after-death is 'NOTHING'
> accept Lord Mother/Father
> the briefness of this life you've granted
> this bliss

*

blueberry bushes, fruit shrunken, dried,
hot july day, outside this window moving

that leaning tree is static as we move away
vanish in its distance
won't be here the day it falls
or the bushes return again to bloom
sitting in a room on wheels
takes us
          Pacific Ocean to the Great Lakes
middle passage the explorers dreamed of
                                                            died for
past the scattered daisies in the green ditches,
the drowning forests, bursting water-lilies,
sun-lit glades

*

mile what?
a lack of notation
reaching for conclusions
tho none are there
you get the green forest
red dying leaves
off-white of the drowned birches
leaves you wondering what it is ends
or is it only an endless renewal
God my life ends
years before this poem possibly can

*

as night falls
it all falls

the sky gradually caves in
becomes the same still darkness as the trees

well past dusk
the husk of night's broken only by the train's light
stars & moon out of sight behind the clouds' wall
contains us in this cave
in whose mouth lie rumours of our shadows
other worlds round other suns
dim flicker of light
visible suddenly across the lake
before the train takes us round the bend
into the illusory dark

*

is this the poem i wanted to write?

it never is

its a thing of words
construct of a conscious mind

governed by the inevitable end-rime
time

*

that's the tone

buried in the poem
a consciousness of its own mortality

or mine

a finality Homer

soon there's noone knows
whether your poem's your own

or if the name denoted a community of speakers
history of a race

(Ellie's an obvious we
draws our child's breath & her own)

i's a lie
dispenses illusions of plot

biography when geography's the clue
locale & history of the clear <u>you</u>

*

who to, Nicky?

only the future
invisible as my own

our first child died
this second waits its birth

all part of history
all what we call a life

echoes & screams thru these tunnels of trees
running on tracks we no longer perceive

Ellie asleep in the lower berth
voices & footsteps move all night
along the moving corridors of the train

*

mist again at dawn

heading into Toronto
'end' translates 'home'

7 a.m.
August 2nd
1981

St Clair to Union Station
thru the junkyards, the backyard gardens,
decaying brick factories

scrawled across the one wall
I WANTED TO BE AN ANARCHIST

an ending
in itself
unending

Vancouver to Toronto
July 27th to August 2nd
1981

Book IV

INCHOATE ROAD

I

1

in Choate Road
a car stalled
underneath the bridge i
pass over
another fragment

water spill
the frozen spume of
the river
                    runs thru Port Hope
into

winter storm across the lake's imperfect ice
blue gaps in the clouds & snow
older worlder order
o der wrld er wrl o
inchoate world

2

life like lake like
                                line
                                        lingers
a dream of
ocean and
pacific one i was born by
bounded in that first family
superior as the other shore
crossing the land bridge between
ocean-going vessels steaming into
both ports i
was there
                    sea to sea
all i needed was
to let the water take me
home

3

i was taught it as
their history
                    but it made sense:

1 if by land
                    (you can make it on foot)
2 if by sea
                    (i need
a boat
            to carry me
                              OUT
                                          THERE

4

water music

two rivers
winding thru

Winnipeg

ocean & lake

what our music
                    our poems come
down to
            the sea in

'everything gives way &
nothing stays fixed'

'the river shines
between the villages'

two translations

see how they wind
this way & that

this name or
another

tracking me

5

'for other waters are
continually flowing on'

& other songs

emptying out

spring into stream into river into lake into
ocean
'n ocean 'n
ocean
'n ocean 'n
ocean
'n ocean 'n
ocean

6

in Choate Road
the cars go by
exhaust blue
late january frost

i thot the water spill
a broken mill
going too fast &
couldn't quite connect it

the image

& beyond that
the town &
beyond that the lake &
beyond that

7

this is the world

not these words

not this poem

this is the world

II

1

snow out the window's light
glimmer's outline
ships, a bay
(anchored)

across this page
a light moves
in the water's now
wet blackness of the street
empty stretches snowy beach
reach as far as i can see into the darkness around this bay

window'd prairie sky
empty hole dug
makes a pond the city will not let them put water in &
then the tree 'n trees
mark the twisting course of

these lines stretch across a country   a life   snow falls   birds &
i grow older with every word
every liquid gesture flows from this blue pen   watermarks
mark time
my life by
the side of
this bodies these

2

beginning with lead & wood
mark the course of this writing's later
ink as the words begin to flow

late   rink lights coming on
shouts of the kids on the frozen water &
later   th'aw
flooding spring
hot stretches of summer
falls
        ice/water
        ice/water
        ice

3

pigeons on the track, a rack
ing cough ing
breath's frozen face

mouth of the assiniboine/red
(river)(brick)(engine of the train)
under the bridge the birds
nest along the top ledge of
abandoned factory across the river to
St Boni face to face
with memory at the mere's edge
more'n merely water goes
one into the other
                                        (seen from the plane) those
alphabets these
rivers
            strokes of
pens together in the plain
words   dried ink   dyes
strained thru   books
the stain of thinking
the rivers the
type we were
down at the mouth
where the two come together

watching our breath
lines of trees
track across the river tracks we was
thinking of writing
vast expanse of white twisting no

4

not so much that but this

not so much then but now

not so much beginnings but beginning

again's a gain

a river arrive
air ver-y cold &

the drift

under the stillness
the silent stretches
a current accrues
air collide us

not so much the river but the riven
moment (more meant to you than

then this

5

out window the light
damned width of the river's length
twists thru the mountains
clouds   just below the tops
twist too the two
wind thru &

                        the river's
ever varied very song the
birds & the snow & the
very hush of the damned world goes
dawn & on   ocean   river
                    lake   stream

i was in river

i was lost in lake

i was caught in the twist &
toss in the water

                              (essential's pull
                              these pools
                              perception
falls

all's a damn now
a pulsated
full)

o
  'n tary
o
  'n hurry
o
  ' linger

  (so that these rhythms are established
   closure (details -- what we call a
   theme) globular, returning, the
   circumnavigation of
   the work/world
o)

  'cean 'n stay
o
  'n go
o-ke-an-o
winds thru the poem the
words say slower & slower the
eaupen measure of

(i stood at the edge of o & e

a u (au -- 'to') the translation where
e goes in these
l'eau countries

6

in the snow world
slowed wheels rumble
the heaped flow of the crystals grow
around us
white's white shift
slips thru the hung trees
line the slopes of these mountain valleys &
we drift on as the snow mounts
higher climbing
towards an imagined top or ridge
entrances the cloud world hid
to the fall now
thru snow, white clouds
the world be/l'eau

7

o eau (eaucean)

o world (lake
river, path the vowels take
to the sea)

eau io
i 'nvoke you
sometimes

why?

o beginning gaining
vision of the water
births you int'
o

wave of speech
sound sine g

s-ing
ing
mouther
sonne
farther

INK o it
!*whirl*!

8

giggle mesh

looking for the place the puns flesh out
the body of speech is
re vealed, the veil
drops away
the dance!
sheer ecstasy of glimmering
part icles part airy
nothingnessence
flow of grammar hammers in
my chest, the breath's pressed OUT
quick liquid spout of
the wail:
THOT
a kind of harbour or

land
and m and no
places the eyes rest
flat/calm/march/day
-- still snow still --
(did i expect it to blow away?)

---

pair of dice
-adox
pay the price &
get your change

'do you have exact change?'
i can only approximate

---

vapour

how the words (the selves) twist
every chance you take

water
watair

(dew
dawn
deer on the lawn below me
river rushes &
clouds &

(water rodes
the passes: the
rocks & twists of
river bubbling up from
earth falling
emptying out (somewhere)
beyond

water
int'
a i 'r
o

III

river riven

wandering the length up & down
when was it i

---

quoted myself
into the world

1

word'l get you world

flood of feeling

when the river
overflows its banks
mudder
no fodder now

floating away in a boat from the house
Winnipeg 1950
that fall we nailed a donkey to the wall
just below the window on the second floor
to mark how high the water'd risen

flood was the word i learned
& rain & river, water
drove me out of my world
mother/father
into another

2

ech-

eau

vo-cab-u-lar-y

diction airy or
at best suspect

flood

mud

(wreck

row)

two rivers known
two more as the summer comes & goes

Red Assiniboine
Saskatchewan Bow

wryme

old wyrm
ouroboros

i-row-ny
(set out in a pun t'
cross this
sudden sea)

3

the trick is to know the depth always
& that the surface'll get you there

the flood'll bring the bottom to the top

spins & the spinner marks the spot
the line drops down

the hook's only visible when
you get more than your feet wet

rhy-
wry thm
    theme

two in-
separable
tune

leer ich
(sneer 'i')

trance forms
within you (around you)

dusk rain on the harbourfront
from the café chair
gulls gulled
i am engulfed, flooded with
même mer, 'e says, or
the same more 'e
experienced be-
fore

feelings flow
like a river
the river flowed
like a river at flood tide
watch the lake rise
rainy august night
or maybe ordinary
like a jewel eye
glittering in a real face
sudden surprise of the place
the distraction of resemblances

-- in land sea
-- under ground river
-- fire water
-- air stream

wa of birth
of water
waltz

wan
(one

(singular ich's istence))

along a rain-pocked river
across this rain-pocked lake

sea
be { gan
gins
a gain

air ' rain
'n a trance later
two in one
wanders the flood
plain

5

among the bushes
the brush the
rushes the
different rivers i followed the courses of
-- Assiniboine, Red, Seine, Neebing, McIntyre, Kaministiqua --
some i knew the proper names of
we called them all 'the river'

heading upstream
tracking the beaver dams
flooded bush
collecting bullrushes for
my mother fell
full face in the mud

slow meander of sludge brown water swam in
shit drifting by
sewage from the towns lay south of us

learned those names for water
(sky aspect -- storm --
intermixed with elemental fire
the sign for 'loud noise')
understood the local & the universal
but moved too often to make the local my own

i was born from water
bore me away from home
again & again after i was born

6

'i should've been a sailor'

wasn't

7

the contradiction is
to spend your life on land
trance fixed in
the sea

contra the diction is
the land wage
(when the water comes
-- sea pun -- you pay a
price)
          pays

                    flood

                    flawed

                    flowed

                              (how you move from
                              imperfection to imperfection in
                              the world)

my body is water
my life is water
ich
eau ech
eau
eau

8

ink eau
ate world

our obra is
the water works
hydro eclectic

tide ties me in this flux
the surface   change is
constantly

when the flood resided
i saw we'd lived
under the sea
all those years

i never saw it til
water covered me
clouds blew by
sea 'n
folds of fields appeared in air
i saw the saints there
& here &

i think in ink
particle charged airs
hum
anity
in
anity
an ity world a
pen opens
floods over me

i write from the bottom of a see
step out upon the surface
poetic feet give me access to
stare cases
& where that leads me
floods the white plain page is
ground/sea/sky

                    inchoate world
                            words

seaquence

            'the way', we say,
            'the letters lie'

EPILOGUE

35,000 feet above Saskatchewan
less than a foot between me &
all that air, these airs err
insubstantial as comparison
spots to which we come, position ourselves
heirs to the veaucabulairies
terrer that fires us
all gollems finally
someone marks our foreheads
four elements there
                    we lurch forward
enact tradition
                monstrously
familiair
            familheir
tri bull
            labyrinthinemine
a tour of
gnossos
logos
osos
    (o that s.o.s. of
consciousgnoss)

or that old question
'who's the boss?' (b.s. os)

minos most of our memory
we function out of loss
amigos

              unless i've got a pun
i can't write it down

ink think

'is that what you mean by procoss?'
(harbour lights
th'arbor of masts &
sails off the edge of your world   a view
venue   sTREEtS
lower&upper
middle voice/tongue/world)
i mean the earthyear the puns get the more the pen can pin it down to

Pan plays the world 'pon his flute

old bullfoot amazes us
pipes bright as language

                                  sleepy giants
who will wake you
mourn your death &
dance your resurrection

                                dreaming world
(the rivers branch like
trees
              someone's always leaving

(catch in the voice the
ship

              water water water you
              doing?

(meme eau: i'm just looking at the sea 'n world
                                                                  (eauver & eauver)))
something fishy when the tongue slips

(glimmering surface
invisible depths
across which the boats skip)

'I'll write you a letter'
(A to A))

giant talk

the long waged war
the fight or struggle for
the mind
                boarders in these rooms words open

i said that be

you said that be

we said that be } FORE

they said that be

warned

                    letting the future know
                  we're playing thru
                  gulf the gulls & mist rise out of
                  stretches between 'me' & 'you'

Book V

IN THE PLUNKETT HOTEL

The Travellers' Home
Away from Home

Our Aim is to Please
Our Patrons

Phone:
Viscount, No. 38 ring 4

Plunkett Hotel

Mrs. W. Workman
Proprietress

At Your Service

Dray Service Second to
None!

FEED STABLE
in connection.

Phone:
Viscount No. 38 ring 4,

W. Workman

Plunkett, Sask.

In the Plunkett Hotel
stairs creak all night
the prairie grass
beyond the shivering glass & the windowframe
rustles
            train rushing by
& the dust, the air,
move in thru the pub's open door
this man asking us
'you Walt & Ag Workman's kids' kids?'
& we were/are
blood is the line you write thru history
shows thru
he knew them
stayed in the hotel too
1932 he said or 33

from the Plunkett Hotel
i watch the solitary car turn beneath me in the street
the kids who
drinking in the bar all night
eventually bought some roadies
took off
                returning now
parking
the train rolls by
stops near where the station used to be
& the kids take off again
                                returning home
unlike me

in the Plunkett Hotel
climbing the narrow stairs
sleeping where grandma & grandpa did
'i think this is the original bed'
rooms rented
ten fifty a night
'if they made any improvements
i can't see what they did'
i is trying to come home
i piles i's bags on the bedside table
i lives there

from the Plunkett Hotel
walking up the street
my sister Dea, her husband & kids,
this family tree
branch begun in Saxony Germany
eighteen thirty-
nein
ja
seems to me
i take the ja way
everytime i admit this history
gaze over tracks into fields & trees
prayer 'e made 'n
(e's me
(ease me thru
to truth or true
conclusion)
i'm mi
i is simply
mind in motion
instances in i's notion)
singing 'ifamly
fiamly
faimly
family
famliy
famlyi'

in the Plunkett Hotel
my grandmother, Agnes Leigh,
made the beds, cooked the meals
day after day for
the commercial travellers stayed there
& her husband, Walter Workman,
ran the dray service
stabled the horses
fed them water, hay &
raised kids
welcomed them when they came back again
as they did
til the hotel was sold
1941
& we are only travellers when we return
customers for someone else to serve

from the Plunkett Hotel
my mother moved out   into the world
returning here
                                        her first few children born
this is where she went when she went 'home'
none of the content remains
only the frame
like Great Grandpa Casper's house
out there in the midst of that muddy field
we stood in the wind & rain
Great Uncle Fred telling me
'that's where you ma was born'
no road or path to lead us there
over the dark furrowed stretches of that earth

from the Plunkett Hotel
the roads run everywhere
arbitrary centre
soul heir
in no way we could ever plan it
we orbit there
spin out
centres for some other we never see
Great Grandpa Casper
dead fifteen years before Ma ever thot of me
Great Grandma Sarah
fifteen years before him
we stood over there graves in the little graveyard
by the side of Route 16
Dea & me
these family plots
more layered than we'd like to believe
leaf
                    these femme Leigh trees

in the Plunkett Hotel
no trace remains of what my grandparents did
-- the building painted, walls papered --
only the memory of conversations
Dea & i
as kids had with
grandma, ma, of what went on
in this building, these streets,
little you can use now to feed a story
-- only the name, a few people in town --
most of us drive by or
tear down someone else's history
(drove 20 miles to show Dea the house where Ellie was born
'torn down only the week before'
don't give me that shit about the old home town)
some few photos we hang onto
as keepsakes

from the Plunkett Hotel
the roots run everywhere:
Minnesota (where my grandparents met);
Vermont (where my mother's mother's mother came from);
England (where Walt's father came from);
Saxony (where Casper's dad was born);
or Toronto, where Ellie & i met,
Saskatoon, where ma & pa were married,
Burnaby, (where they were living when they had me) --
the me runs everywhere
like a theme
moving reservoirs of cells & genes
stretches out over the surface of the earth
more miles than any ancestor ever dreamed
we trace our dreamtime in blood,
the colour of an eye, line of a chin,
say 'you remind me of your grandpa' or
'you do that just the way my mother did',
tribal, restless, constant only in the moving on,
over the continents
thru what we call our history
tho it is more mystery than fact,
more verb than noun,
more image, finally, than story

in the Plunkett Hotel
we became what we really are,
transient, temporal, i's in motion
crossing the flickering division lines of history
(our own history incomplete
(more oral than written))
moved by love
                    by longing
by fear of what that love contains --
possessive, passionate,
original, consuming,
all part of
                finally
a state of mind
                        the real
                        the only borders of
                        my kind

July 1st to October 23rd 1983

Book VI

THE GRACE OF THE MOMENT

Saint: From the latin *sanctus*, 'holy', the name
applied initially to all Christians..."

JCJ Metford, *Dictionary of Christian Lore And Legend*

the grace of the moment

or the necessity
to live each minute
as i was taught always
to catch it

the real ride is the present tide
pulls you   out
mark the me's
mar or are the sub
stance or text of
a life.

so that even <u>this</u> vocabulary
changes with the pull of present
words entering the ear or eye
their current's currency
carries them
into the unmapped reaches of your future
poem

'let's not bring that up'
'i'm too tired to discuss it'
'there's certain things we never mention'
'you show good form when you don't talk about it'

like politics or
the subjective voice or

all the awkward feet that don't fit
the antholegaic voice of the poetry biz
the feverish alliteration of the fake fucks

no st. algia here
just the bare longing of the moment lingers

mo' me(a)nt (or in the instant 'means')
the tense switches
(that fast) i can never fix it

donkey tricks

i wear this language
like a bag of feed

a dictionary
dangling from a stick

the damn nouns & verbs
let's just say i love you

digestion
(consumed by desire by
time) 'i feel a poem coming on'
like a song or
attack of gas
fuels your flight from past
into the dizzying present of the future

moment & airy in st ant's perception
'I'd equate it thus -- X + Y
-- present's plus
pre-sentiment we see it clearly
minus any consciousness of the heart's toll
i know we flee into the endless nattering of soul-
searching'   evade the moment
(imprecision of the term
in which the verb 'to write' is served)

absolute absolute
*a b*rief *s*oliloquy *on lute*
'music in the moment'
precision of the notion second
first time never is observed
head flashing back on itself like a record
a record of itself flashing back like a head
'i thot it was the heart with which we were concerned'

Donna
dead of cancer   October 21st, 1983
cousin born the same year as me
carried my dead sister's name
death brackets endlessly
being ing be finally that aside
that drop in voice
notated in
death's presence
the dread flicks past
all light & motion
a film by Renoir
a painting or
a building
       if Wren were still alive
saint
    one you roll over
    gather this moss or leave them
    two: the daily rise & fall of hierarchies

dog days

we carry the red ribbons mark us for death
the blood of being flooding out or
leeched
      brief bright ribbon we wrap the present in
      this human grace

saint saint
's ain't nothin' but what it is
tongue of consciousness upon the face
licked awake
dream world sank t' us
sunken world we walk thru
at land is the lost level of our lives
the 'easily gotten mystery image' any life assumes
longing for distant surfaces
forgotten coasts & harbours
lovers in some other room

the lips & limbs articulated
made whole, holy in that sense,
sanctus sanctuary
hidden within the bright tangles of the body

bright, praise,
how these initials craze us
dog our feet
                    give us the right to raise our voices
speak
           's a peak the tongue reaches
beyond because
the tongue exceeds the grasp
rasps against the flesh &
we shudder
down

what good do they do?
these words to mourn the death of others?
this talk of love?

you take the in door st. ant
                                        sunk
opening we thunk as hope
the dead dead
cancer worms & time tormented or
rapturous   carried   briefly   beyond
into a something
marked as cliche

                         we mourn nontheless
thrust into insistence by the pressure of a life
a death
              miss you/miss you/miss you
              cannot stop this insistent act

of breath

of speech

each line a life
everything resides in

                              we are lief
                                        unlucky
                                                  cast up on this shore
the new found land another age longed for

taken as familiar
granted
the given returns
taunts us
a taste on the tongue
undone by the momentary pleasures of the flesh

give in   dig
est ion or any other particle or question
just ation
a jest or
je saint
that same vari
very minor note
daily or sailyent point a ship reaches
vinland or
inland dreams of oceans too wide to cross
lost in the turn & toss
the beloved's body

catalogues
(dogalogues)
di in the very tac God takes
against the windy breath of
these songs
becalmed in the vast reaches of the world
to find belief & a way back home   away

(too wakeful to sleep
y to wake
lines run
from the mind to
the pen
the tongue
say love or
plunge
into a bitter world of beasts
demons or
a moral
stance assumed
can i take it too
sing that 'wake me when the damned show up' tune?

or me?
locate the pro
noun my life becomes
work my life assumes?)

it is all personal
all person &
per the son that dies
still born or
the son you never were but wore
caught in th' e
lips is <u>life</u>...lived, as it were,
out of tune
                    two 'n one or
in one   door & out the other
voices speaking
that this suffering is born in language
that that is true & that that is true
two true or
wholly to be believed but
who'll y' find to
believe it?
                    leave it
this pain words wear
carry within them like a spine
involves the very line its
twists & turns

we say it burns
it hurts
             the body aches
             the heart breaks
we are dumbed or numb
inarticulate in the face of it
rhyme badly
search for metaphors
when what it is is the world
that noun   that thing
upon which (within)
this singing is the small instance of a being
holy alive
& holey
                 wholly here

we all want the same thing   which is always different   the 'other'
escape this flesh &
lose ourselves or loose
even as we stepped outside our parents' bodies
as our daughters step
even as the walls become waltz become
'wish i knew that two-step too'
into one makes one makes
three me's & three i's &
three we's we're not alone
living in a mystery
echoey   shadowy
mi fa
mily so--
these difficult musics
the muse sticks to

s makes the comic cosmic
heaven sheaven
drunk on the i's dea of paradise
i deal
shuffle off this mortal coil
(double helix or hex --
reverse conjunctions where a life's made
mad   ('s cream
(milk it for all its worth)))

the problem's to connect in the first place, establish how the flux creates the fax, that if our experience of 'now' is (essentially) illusory -- an amalgalm of light particles & a variable ability to anticipate a sequence of future activities -- then these flix of consciousness fix it accurately: what Wittgenstein saw (hence his use of the file card); Stein's insistent insistence (tracking the way the syntax flexes); McLuhan's sense of the thot probe --

'Appreciation, however, lags behind, partly owing to the inherent nature of this art. People read instead of looking; paradoxically, because letters are so familiar people do not know what they really look like.'
[Nicolette Gay in *The Painted Inscriptions of David Jones*]
tone

t' one ton e carries on its
tongu   life
that old BLUES moan
dedicates the real weight of speech

'he weighs every word'
'he's accurate to the letter'
'he's always prompt with his letters'
'answer that letter or you're out of work'

now now now now now
stammering accurate speech
occupies the present
's past
a spa st's go to
last blessings
last writes
death tracks the very life he rites
writ large
                    that letter of
                    the law   waltz

                                        just you
                                        & the language too

this business of process
nothing more than
the moment's grace

October 1983 thru January 1984

AFTER BIRD
(improvising)

'to let fly high/let
that bird go, see how yur hand
takes up the space so itself
without the bird crampd in it.'

bill bissett

3.

no ah then
just code

ark de triomphe

the rain bowed
like a fiddle

like a vial in a storm tossed sea

sharp as a hill
from which the dove will   fly out   into the blue
bird   did   (world)

4.

'just some notes
 i wanted to give you'

new/tra/la

'you mean--'
& it is all in tension

sweet viola, lets!

o sax!
o phone!

all this ringing in of changes
chords i get tangled in

this { very
communic } ation

this ear
this earth
this song

1.

little flight
                                                        angle

                            what i 'eard

being then
                                              or not

           f m 'er all at
           once
                        twice

faster than the humming   word
honey
                 bee/ing's sing

all that code
ah that muse
ic'll stick'll

new little light
fangle

                          what i?

                          what ur?

2. (for Robin Blaser)

born { into / on the wings of

how do i / how did i } tie this all together { do you?

i mean the lodged / the bass } ic

line

---

gets drawn

out

robin

like a wormmmmmmmm hmm?

after the rain?
after the rain?
after the rain?
after the rain?
after the rain?

5.

only the lips
and what spills from them

like a beak or
what's in back of the rote
learning

the spare o's
the blue j's

and how they cluster then
in these white remnants of the trees

turn the leaves
over

page after page

calling

6.

wholly book

wholly bird

wholly & always
completely itself

fragile

easy to lose
what a line meant
's there
                    it is
                                  there
      it is
                    there

7.

me
an' i

'ng

(i ambient

eye

ear

)

but then of course i is always rushing in &

think
say
be
sing } ing

8.

sky

wind

cloud

bird

wanted nothing more than that

bird song

wanted that

nothing more then

Most of *Book 6 Books* has appeared previously. Thanks to the following publishers & periodicals: Camrose Review, Canadian Broadcasting Corporation, Canadian Literature, Capilano Review, Credences, Cross-Country, CVII, Dandelion, Gray Matters, Island, Island Press, Labrys, Malahat Review, Oolichan Books, Poetry Toronto, Rampike, Rubicon, Simon Fraser University English Dept, What, Writing.

The music in *The Grace of the Moment* was transcribed by Renwick Day. *Hour 19* was part of a commisioned work for the Elmer Isler Singers entitled *Mating Time*, music by John Beckwith. The music in *Hour 24* is the music of the spheres as worked out by Kepler, with the exception of the last piece which is a notation of the notes not included within Kepler's pattern (done in the pattern of Kepler).The two ads in *In the Plunkett Hotel* originally appeared in The Viscount Sun, Friday, February 8, 1929.

Quotations in this text are both real & imagined. Their point is not to push the reader out into other works (in a search for 'additional depth' as it were) but rather the texture, modulation of tone &/or authority they lend to the work in hand. But with a nod towards rabid curiosity I'll mention a few sources. The third quotation in *Hour 4* is from Jack Vance's *The Languages of Pao*. The quote attributed to Archy in *Hour 6* is, of course, from Dom Marquis' *Archy and Mehitabel*, the quoted fragment following it from the Mary Jane and Sniffles stories in *Looney Tune Comics*, & the 'turtle' fragment from Ogden Nash's famous poem. The first & last quotation in *Hour 9*, & the poem quoted in the middle of it, are all from the first American edition of Kenneth Grahame's *The Wind in the Willows*. The first three quotations in *Hour 14*, and the second last one, are from the writings of Wang Wei. The quotations in *Inchoate Road* Part I poems 4 & 5 are from Heraclitus, Wang Wei & Heraclitus respectively; in Part III the opening 'quote' is actually a paraphrase of part of Cid Corman's translation of Basho's *Back Roads To Far Places*. Other writers' lines are echoed & quoted thruout *The Martyrology Book 6 Books*. Compositional dates refer to the dates within which the first complete draft of the relevant text was completed. Revisons continue up to the point of publication & occasionally beyond. *The Martyrology Book 7* is envisioned as a boxed, unbound text. *Book 8* will occur among it. Occasional bits of Canada Council & Ontario Arts Council money assisted in freeing time for the writing of parts of this work for which much thanks. Particular thanks too to Frank Davey who has gotten me going again on *The Martyrology* twice now: once in 1974 with a comment on Louis Dudek's work that launched me into *Book 4*; again in 1978 when i had barely begun *A Book of Hours* & an observation he made put the work on track. And finally, much thanks to Fred Wah who told me to shut up & keep writing.

bpNichol
Toronto July 31, 1986

A Note on Reading

All spacing in The Martyrology is deliberate, including the variable spacing at tops and bottoms of pages, and should be read as part of the rhythm of the poem.

Canadian Cataloguing in Publication Data

Nichol, B.P., 1944-1988
The martyrology, book 6: 1978-1985

Facsimile ed.
Poems.
ISBN 0-88910-319-4

I. Title.
PS8527.I32M34 1994 C811'.54 C93-093594-2
PR9199.3.N52M3 1994

Design input by Stan Bevington, bpNichol, Jerry Ofo and Gordon Robertson. Keyed on a variety of personal computers and LaserWriter typeset by Mary Scally.
The paper is acid-free Zephyr Antique laid. First printed in January 1987 in an edition of 750 copies. Another 500 copies were printed in November, 1994 as a gift to the spirit of bp by the printers at the old Coach House, 401 Huron Street, on bpNichol Lane, Toronto.